The Painted Garden Cookbook

An Illustrated Collection of Homegrown Recipes

Written and illustrated by

Mary Woodin

RUNNING PRESS
PHILADELPHIA · LONDON

Dedication

For my parents, Charles and Susanne Woodin, with love

9 8 7 6 5 4 3 2 1

Digit on the right indicates the number of this printing

Library of Congress Control Number: 2009929921

ISBN 978-0-7624-3835-8

Cover and interior design by Corinda Cook

Edited by Kristen Green Wiewora

Typography: BeLucian, Corinthia, Goudy, and Univers

Running Press Book Publishers
2300 Chestnut Street
Philadelphia, PA 19103-4371

Visit us on the web!
www.runningpress.com

Contents

Acknowledgements

Biggest thanks of all, of course, go to my husband Andrew for keeping the family show on the road while I have been incarcerated in my studio, and to my children Saskia, Reuben, and Fifi for their patience when I have been too busy writing a cookbook to dish up dinner on time.

I have also greatly appreciated all the help and inspiration I have had from family and friends along the way, from recipe-testing and tasting to relentless weeding, and for good ideas with stubborn ingredients. Thank you, Sarah and Derek Stevens; Ruth Stevens; Deborah Glass Woodin; Mum and Dad; the Graham family; Lara Brown; Nicky Jacobs; Bridget McIntyre; Helen—with a little help from Oliver and Alex—Pearson; Grace Watts; Mary Crawford; Margaret O'Byrne; Lynda, Jess, and Jack Leslie; Stephanie Burridge; Dan and Henrietta Neuteboom; Fern Mackour; and Joanna Trythall.

This book started with the seed of an idea, and I am indebted to Lucy, Stephanie, and Alex at The Artworks for so enthusiastically believing in that idea, and making it happen from there on.

Thanks also to all the team at Running Press, especially Kristen Green Wiewora for her patient answering of all my questions, and Corinda Cook for her beautiful and sensitive design work.

Cook's notes

The initial inspiration for this book was the excitement of being able to cook with the freshest of ingredients. Apart from your own backyard, farmer's markets offer a good selection of seasonal fruit and vegetables, or look out for locally grown produce in the grocery store. The recipes in this book are designed to be guidelines: no two vegetables are exactly the same so be prepared to prod and taste as you go along, get to know your oven, and adjust cooking times if necessary. I use naturally raised meats, free from antibiotics, whenever possible, along with farm-fresh eggs from my own chickens. Seeking out better ingredients always results in better, healthier food.

Foreword

Four years ago we moved to the country, and we started a fruit and vegetable garden. That is how this cookbook came about. It is a collection of recipes of the sort of food I like to eat, bolstered by—or in some cases, entirely consisting of—the fruits of my labors: simple dishes that make the most of fresh, seasonal food. I still get excited by each seed that germinates, and I love the conundrum of what to cook from an armful of freshly gathered produce. Fortunately, farmer's markets have made that possible for everyone, even if your own gardening exploits extend no further than a pot of basil on the kitchen windowsill!

My background is as an artist; I recorded all the flowers in our London garden in watercolors. There, I battled with tree roots and slugs and foxes, and the irises struggled to bloom behind the football goal. I cosseted a few herbs, grew tomatoes in pots, planted a damson tree and made two pots of jam! Increasingly though, we felt this flirtation with gardening needed space to stretch its wings. We relocated to a Suffolk farmhouse with three acres of garden. With fruit and vegetables added to the equation, my sketchbooks rapidly became recipe notes. Fresh produce has a depth of flavor that requires minimal fuss. Simple seasonal dishes speak for themselves. The fun comes with creating happy combinations, or cooking the same vegetable, day in, day out, but in new and inventive ways.

I am the product of gardeners, and it seems to run in the family. My parents have been cultivating the same soil for fifty years. My childhood garden was largely given over to growing fruit and vegetables, and it still is. I wasn't a very enthusiastic helper: gathering strawberries was the best job, because you could pick and eat; gooseberries were delicious too, but prickly; forking manure felt heroic, but collecting stones was just irksome. We had to be paid to do that. Funny how the chickens come

home to roost; I love all those jobs now, and feel privileged to be able to tinker away in our own productive garden. Some days it's disheartening: the tomatoes get blight, a deer nibbles the broad beans, or the parsnips fail to germinate, but usually there's something to pick, and cook, so I'm happy.

Occasionally I venture from my country nest back to the city. Recently it was to discuss ideas for this cookbook with my agents, Lucy and Steph: we enjoyed a fabulous lunch in Soho, the heart of hustle and bustle. I arrived home late, greeted by the silence of a moonlit night. A frog sat in the middle of the path looking straight at me. I can only imagine he was waiting for a kiss. . . . I had returned to the fairy tale.

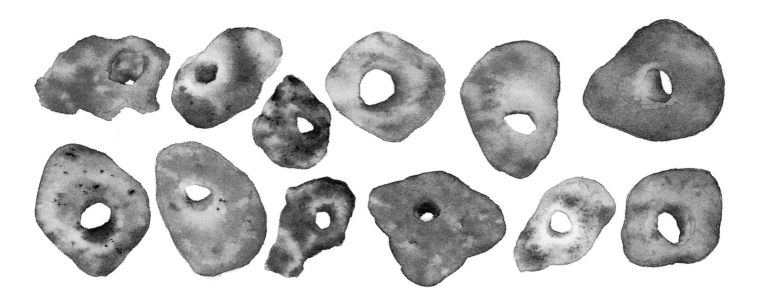

Spring

"Gratitude is the fairest blossom which springs from the soul."

—Henry Ward Beecher, 1813-1887

I love spring.

The days are lengthening, the garden promises so much and my favorite flower, the iris, is almost in bloom. The greenhouse gets a scrub, and the manure heap is dug into the bean trenches. I make long "to do" lists and promise that this year I will keep on top of things. While my back is turned the knee-high froth of new growth suddenly brushes my shoulders. I catch bind weed climbing up the stinging nettles, a gentle reminder I need to be up at six every morning to keep pace. To add insult to injury, the irises have been blown over.

However, the weather is still unpredictable: we have been known to build snowmen at Easter, and after half an hour's weeding in temperatures only just above freezing, I scuttle indoors for hot porridge. It's only when the House Martins return to their nests in the eaves that it feels as though summer is around the corner.

The plum trees are the first to blossom, followed by the apples and pears. Surrounding our garden are commercial orchards, neat rows of apple trees which are a haze of the palest pink and white.

Then seed sowing begins in earnest. The greenhouse is adjacent to my studio, so I sneak in several times a day to check for signs of germination. Once again the seed catalogues have cast their seductive spell, so I will be looking for nooks and crannies in the flower beds for space for the odd cucumber tripod, or fringe of magenta mountain orach.

We've had just a trickle of eggs over the winter, and now all the chickens should be laying; however, it's not all smooth sailing. The bantams have gone broody, sitting tight on their nests in hopes of hatching chicks, and Gabriella has been hiding

her eggs again. Weeding under a clump of day lilies, I discover a clutch of a dozen; a week later, I am out scouring the garden again, looking for her new hiding place. She's dangerously close to being shut in the pen for a day to repent!

Apart from the egg hunts, it's great to be gathering new shoots in the vegetable garden for cooking. There are tender spinach leaves, tiny new potatoes, and the first of a long season of lettuces. If I keep sowing every couple of weeks, we can be eating salad until the first frosts.

Spring

Side Dishes and Starters

Herbed Mousse with Crisp Radishes

Warm Chicken Liver Salad

New Potato and Radish Salad

Carrots and New Potatoes in Marsala

Broccoli and Walnut Gratin

Phyllo-Wrapped Broccoli

Zucchini and Roasted Garlic Soup with Herbed Croutons

Creamy Shredded Zucchini

Warm Beet Salad

Mains

Zucchini Fish Cakes

Zucchini and Pesto Pizza

Spinach and Egg Florentine Pizza

Pasta with Sugar Snap Peas and Salmon

Posh B.L.T. s

Lamb Shanks with Red Wine and Raisins

Desserts

Baked Rhubarb

Crisp Butter Biscuits

Pink Tea Party Meringue-Cream Sandwiches

Sundries

Pizza Dough

Basic Bread

Mayonnaise

Anchovy Mayonnaise

Honey-Mustard Vinaigrette

Rhubarb Curd

Herbed Mousse with Crisp Radishes

Simply scrubbed clean and dipped into a creamy, herbed mousse, young radishes jazz up a salad lunch. Scallion Breadsticks (page 132) are also nice alongside.

Serves 4 to 6

1 sheet gelatin

5 tablespoons (100 milliliters) half-and-half (or single cream)

5 tablespoons (100 grams) low-fat fromage frais or plain Greek-style yogurt

4 tablespoons chopped soft-leaved fresh herbs (basil, parsley, chives, marjoram, or any combination)

Fine sea salt

About 20 radishes (3 or 4 per serving)

Soak the gelatin sheet in cold water until soft, about 5 minutes.

Heat the half-and-half in a small saucepan over a low heat to just below boiling; remove from the heat. Remove the gelatin from the soaking water and squeeze out any excess water. Add it to the half-and-half, stirring to dissolve.

Let the cream mixture cool slightly, then stir in the fromage frais and herbs. Season to taste with salt, and pour into a pretty serving dish. Chill the mousse in the fridge for 3 to 4 hours.

Wash the radishes well and trim off the leaves, leaving about an inch of the stem. Halve the radishes lengthwise, through the stem.

Serve the mousse with the freshly pulled radishes.

Radishes

I don't spend much time or energy cultivating radishes as they are not very versatile in the kitchen, but it is worth growing a row or two for the sheer pleasure of the first crunch of the season. I tuck a few sowings of Cherry Belle in between rows of garlic, but even a window box will do fine. The young leaves of a radish add a peppery edge to salads, and the crimson roots, if picked while still small, are not overbearingly hot.

Warm Chicken Liver Salad

Nestled in a deep green and fuchsia-pink salad of spicy arugula (what we call "rocket" in the UK) and crunchy radish, these tasty chicken livers are perfect for a late spring al fresco lunch when you might be wishing the weather were not quite so fresco! Serve with some lightly toasted Fresh Tomato and Basil Bread (page 130).

Serves 4

4 handfuls arugula or baby spinach

8 radishes, greens trimmed and discarded, thinly sliced

Roasted Garlic Vinaigrette (page 138), or salad dressing
    of your choice

2 tablespoons olive oil

2 large shallots, finely chopped

2 tablespoons unsalted butter

1 pound (400 grams) chicken livers, sinewy bits removed
    and discarded (see note, page 19), coarsely chopped

2 teaspoons orange marmalade or 1 tablespoon Marsala

1 tablespoon chopped fresh flat-leaf parsley

Divide the arugula among 4 plates and scatter the radish slices decoratively on top. Drizzle with a little vinaigrette, until dressed to your liking.

Heat the olive oil in a large skillet over medium heat. Add the shallots and sauté until softened and translucent, for 5 to 7 minutes. Add the butter to the pan along with the chopped livers and cook for about 10 minutes, turning the livers with a spatula every now and again, until they are nicely browned. (It's important to retain a soft pink center in the liver. Cut through a piece with a knife to check. Overcook the liver and it will soon turn rubbery.) Stir in the marmalade, heat through for a moment, then spoon the livers onto the center of each salad and sprinkle liberally with the chopped parsley.

Note: Prepare the chicken livers by scrupulously cutting out any green or sinewy bits. The green is bile, and very bitter—the tiniest taste will put you off eating liver for a long time.

New Potato and Radish Salad

The first tiny new potatoes of the season have so much flavor that they barely need tampering with, but I do love them paired with wafer-thin slices of peppery radish to set off their sweet earthiness.

Serves 4

1 pound (450 grams) small new potatoes,
  preferably the size of marbles

12 radishes

2 tablespoons olive oil

Fine sea salt and freshly ground pepper

1 tablespoon chopped fresh chives, for sprinkling

Fill a pot with 1 inch of water. Place a steamer insert in the pot and bring the water to a boil. Alternatively, bring a large pot of water to boil.

Rub the skins off the potatoes (they should be so thin they come off in your fingers), then steam or boil them for about 5 minutes, or until easily pierced with a sharp knife. Timing will vary according to the size and freshness of the potatoes. Drain and set aside to cool slightly.

Remove the tops and roots from the radishes, and cut into paper-thin slices.

While the potatoes are still warm, slice the larger ones into ¼-inch slices. Add all the potatoes to a mixing bowl, and drizzle with the olive oil. Stir in the radishes and season with salt and pepper.

Serve while the potatoes still have a lingering warmth, with the chives sprinkled over the top.

Carrots and
New Potatoes in Marsala

Marsala is a Sicilian fortified wine made from locally grown grapes, and is used widely in Italian cooking. Since using it in a rhubarb trifle years ago, I have become a convert. I keep a supply in the pantry and sneak it into all sorts of dishes. In this instance, its rich fruity flavor is beautifully absorbed by the vegetables, which makes it a good accompaniment for fish or chicken.

Serves 4 to 6

14 ounces (400 grams) small carrots, peeled and
halved lengthwise

1½ pounds (700 grams) new potatoes, scrubbed
and unpeeled

4 tablespoons olive oil

4 tablespoons Marsala

2½ cups (600 milliliters) vegetable stock, heated and
kept warm

4 tablespoons coarsely chopped fresh cilantro (coriander)

Coarse sea salt and freshly ground pepper

Preheat oven to 400°F (200°C).

Fill a pot with 1 inch of water and set a steamer insert inside; bring water to boil. Alternatively, bring a large pot of water to boil.

Add the carrots to the pot and steam or parboil until heated through but still quite firm, for about 3 minutes. Drain well.

Meanwhile, cut the potatoes into walnut-size pieces. Put the carrots and potatoes in a large baking dish with enough room to spread in a single layer. Add the olive oil and stir to coat all the vegetables evenly. Add the vegetable stock, the Marsala, and the cilantro, and season with salt and pepper. Stir to combine.

Bake the carrots and potatoes uncovered for 50 minutes, stirring halfway through to ensure that the vegetables brown on both sides. When cooked, most of the liquid will have evaporated, leaving the vegetables glossy and aromatic.

Broccoli and Walnut Gratin

This simple recipe elevates broccoli beyond the role of an accompaniment to perform a glittering act of its own. Look for sprouting broccoli at a farmer's market; it just needs washing, no trimming, you can eat the head, leaf, and stalk. If it's not available, substitute with regular broccoli cut into small florets, or broccoli rabe.

Serves 4

3 tablespoons plain Greek-style yogurt

3 tablespoons low-fat fromage frais or mayonnaise

1 pound (500 grams) purple sprouting broccoli
   or broccolini

4 tablespoons olive oil

¾ cup (50 grams) fine plain breadcrumbs

¼ cup (30 grams) finely chopped walnuts

Fine sea salt and freshly ground pepper

Prepare the sauce by combining the yogurt and fromage frais in a small bowl; stir to blend.

Fill a pot with 1 inch of water and set a steamer insert inside; bring the water to boil. Alternatively, bring a large pot of water to boil.

Add the broccoli and steam or boil until soft, for 6 to 7 minutes; drain well.

While the broccoli is cooking, heat the olive oil in a heavy skillet over medium heat. Add the breadcrumbs and the walnuts and sauté, stirring constantly, for just a couple of minutes, or until the walnuts smell toasty. Remove from the heat immediately. There's only a fine line between crisp and aromatic, and burnt. Season the breadcrumbs to taste with salt and pepper.

To serve as a starter, divide the broccoli among 4 plates, sprinkle with the breadcrumbs, then give each plate a spoonful of sauce on the side.

Purple Sprouting Broccoli

My broccoli crop was decimated by a flock of peafowl this year. Every so often, they cruise down from a couple of fields away and head straight for my vegetable garden. They are beautiful, seductive creatures. I love their rasping call with saxophone overtones, their superior gaze, and, of course, their catwalk couture. I could watch them all day if I didn't care so passionately about my broccoli. So rather than pondering their beauty I am more likely to be seen lurching towards them with my own rasping call.

With its dainty purple heads, deep green leaves, and crunchy stalk, purple sprouting broccoli has much more character than the dense, overgrown green florets found in the grocery store. Purple sprouting broccoli is indigenous to the UK, so if you cannot find it where you are, broccolini or broccoli rabe are good substitutes.

Phyllo-Wrapped Broccoli

The fresh sweetness of sprouting broccoli unites a hint of chile with the buttery crispness of phyllo pastry. This is one to get the taste buds tingling! Chile oil is available in the Asian food section of many supermarkets.

Serves 4

2 tablespoons olive oil

1 tablespoon chile oil, or substitute a finely chopped medium-hot chile

4 large shallots, finely chopped

1 pound (500 grams) sprouting broccoli, any tough stalks trimmed, or broccolini

Coarse sea salt and freshly ground pepper

8 sheets fresh or frozen thawed phyllo pastry

2 tablespoons melted unsalted butter

2 tablespoons plain Greek-style yogurt

2 tablespoons mayonnaise

Preheat the oven to 400°F (200°C). Grease a large baking sheet.

Combine both oils in a large skillet; cover and heat over medium heat. Uncover and add the shallots. Sauté gently for 5 to 7 minutes, until translucent.

Add the broccoli to the pan, stirring to coat evenly with the oil. Add a couple of tablespoons of water. Cover and cook for about 5 minutes, shaking the pan occasionally to prevent any sticking. Remove from the heat while the broccoli is still just slightly undercooked and retains a lovely bright green color. It will be cooked further in the oven, so it should still have a crisp bite. Freshly picked broccoli will cook much faster than broccoli that has been hanging around in the fridge for a few days, so exercise your own judgment here.

Let cool slightly, then season the broccoli with salt and pepper and coarsely chop. Transfer the broccoli to a shallow bowl so that it will be cool enough to handle when the pastry is ready.

On a work surface, quarter each phyllo sheet to yield a total of 32 squares. Keep the stack of phyllo squares covered with a damp cloth or piece of plastic wrap to prevent them from drying out. Working with 4 squares of pastry at a time, brush each one lightly with the melted butter, and stack atop one another. If any squares tear, just use them in the middle layer. Spread a heaping tablespoon of the cooked broccoli in a line about an inch from the bottom, leaving an inch border on either side of the square, and fold the sides over towards the center, just enough to hold the filling in. Roll the whole sheet from the bottom to the top, encasing the broccoli, as you might a burrito or a cylindrical gift wrapped in tissue paper. Place seam-side down on the prepared baking sheet and brush the top of the parcel with the remaining melted butter. Repeat the process with the remaining squares of phyllo, making 8 parcels in all.

Bake until the tops are crisp and golden, about 10 minutes. While they are baking, mix together the yogurt and mayonnaise in a bowl to serve with the parcels.

Zucchini and Roasted Garlic Soup with Herbed Croutons

Flecked with green and seasoned with the subtle caramelized taste of sweet roasted garlic, this smooth, creamy soup is the perfect dish to herald the start of the zucchini season. Choose small, dark-skinned squash that are dense and juicy. Double cream, a very rich British cream, may be available at some fine cheese shops and specialty food stores, but heavy whipping cream works just as well in this recipe.

Serves 4

SOUP

4 tablespoons olive oil

1½ pounds (700 grams) zucchini, cut into ½-inch pieces

2 medium onions, chopped

2 heads roasted garlic, garlic squeezed out of the skins
(see note)

4 cups (900 milliliters) vegetable stock, heated and
kept warm

Fine sea salt and freshly ground pepper

4 tablespoons double cream or heavy whipping cream,
for serving (optional)

CROUTONS

2 tablespoons olive oil

2 thick slices Herb Bread (page 128) or ciabatta, cubed

For the soup: Heat the olive oil in a large skillet over medium heat. Add the zucchini and onions and sauté for 15 minutes, stirring occasionally, until the zucchini is soft and the onion is just beginning to brown at the edges. Transfer the vegetables to a blender. Add half of the warm stock and the roasted garlic and carefully purée until smooth. Alternatively, transfer the vegetables, half of the stock, and roasted garlic to a large saucepan and purée with an immersion blender until smooth.

In a large saucepan, combine the puréed vegetables with the remaining stock and return to the heat to warm through. Adjust seasonings to taste.

For the croutons: Heat the oil in a small skillet over medium-high heat. Add the bread cubes and fry until lightly browned on all sides.

To serve: Pour the soup into 4 bowls and swirl 1 tablespoon of the cream into each serving; top with the croutons.

Note: To roast whole garlic heads, slice about ¼-inch off the top of the garlic bulb, just far enough down to cut the tips off the individual cloves. Place the garlic on a square of foil large enough to encase the whole bulb and drizzle the cut surface of the bulb with 2 teaspoons olive oil. Wrap the foil around the garlic, place in a small baking dish, and roast at 400°F (200°C) for about 30 minutes, until the garlic feels soft when squeezed. Unwrap and let sit until cool enough to handle.

Creamy Shredded Zucchini

If the bounty of your summer zucchini crop is beginning to be met with groans at the table, try this simple side dish, whose texture will just straddle crisp and soft if you keep a close eye on the cooking! The creaminess of this dish goes really well with grilled pork. Any leftovers are perfect for chucking into a frittata for lunch the next day.

Serves 4

1 pound (500 grams) zucchini (3 or 4 small), coarsely grated

3 tablespoons unsalted butter

6 tablespoons (90 milliliters) double cream or heavy whipping cream (optional)

Fine sea salt and freshly ground pepper

1 tablespoon freshly grated Parmesan cheese

Melt the butter in a large skillet over medium heat until foaming. Add the zucchini and cook for 4 to 5 minutes, stirring occasionally. Keep tasting along the way; you want the zucchini to remain just undercooked.

While it still has a nice bite to it, quickly add the cream, if going the indulgent route, and season with salt and pepper. Keep the pan on the stove just long enough to heat the cream through, then transfer the zucchini to a warmed serving dish, sprinkle the Parmesan over the top, and serve immediately.

Note: Double cream is a traditional British treasure with a high butterfat content—around 48 percent. That's higher even than ultra-pasteurized heavy whipping cream, which contains around 38 to 40 percent butterfat. If you cannot find double cream, substitute well-drained crème fraîche for a similar fat content. It's not essential for the health conscious, but adds a certain luxury to the dish. Alternatively, you can substitute heavy whipping cream or half-and-half with no trouble at all.

Warm
Beet Salad

The cool, peppery dressing on this salad tempers the sweetness of the warm beets. Drizzle the yogurt over the chunks of beet just before serving to enjoy the contrast of green, white, and purple. You can substitute ready-cooked beets (avoiding those steeped in vinegar) and warm them through in the oven before chopping. Serve the salad with cold meats or salty slices of broiled halloumi cheese.

Serves 4

4 small beets (about 1 pound or 450 grams)

1 tablespoon extra-virgin olive oil

Fine sea salt and freshly ground pepper

A handful of arugula, about 2 ounces or 50 grams

½ cup (120 grams) plain Greek-style yogurt

Preheat the oven to 325°F (170°C).

Wash the beets well, leaving the roots intact, and trim off the leaves without cutting into the beet itself. Put the beets on a double layer of aluminum foil, drizzle with the olive oil, and season with salt and pepper. Tightly wrap the beets in the foil, place in an ovenproof dish, in case of any leakages, and cook for about 1½ hours, until the beets are soft enough to be pierced with a knife.

While the beets are cooking, pound the arugula to a paste using a mortar and pestle, then briefly swirl it into the yogurt, just until green and white streaks form. Alternatively, you can use a mini food processor to finely chop the arugula, but it won't be quite the same.

Remove the beets from the oven and open the foil package to release the steam. When the beets are still warm but cool enough to handle, rub the skins off the beets, and chop them into 1½-inch chunks. Do wear an apron to protect your clothing from pink splashes. You could also wear kitchen gloves or plastic bags over your hands if you don't wish to stain your fingers.

Place the chopped beets in a serving bowl while they are still warm, and pour the yogurt over the top, letting it meander its way through the crevices.

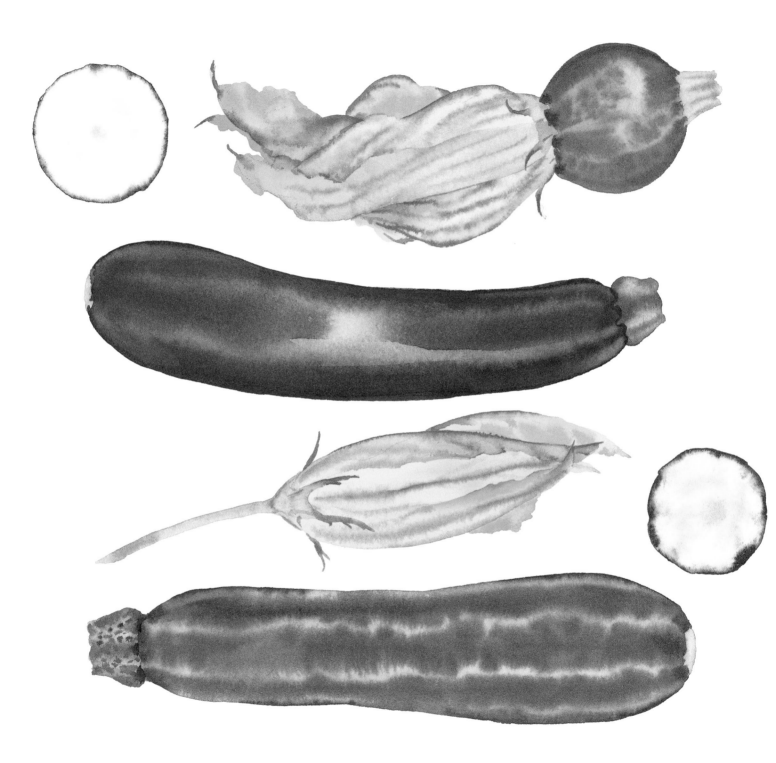

Zucchini Fish Cakes

These cakes are equally good made with mackerel or salmon. Moist and packed full of healthy fats, either fish teams perfectly with the first super-sweet zucchini pickings. Whichever one you use, make sure your fish is fresh and has been responsibly fished. Serve with very lemony mayonnaise that you can whip up at the last minute: simply stir the juice from half a squeezed lemon into a small bowl of mayonnaise, using more or less to taste. You can grate in the zest from the lemon as well for an extra burst of citrus.

Serves 4

2 small zucchini (10 ounces or 300 grams), cut into
    $\frac{1}{8}$-inch cubes

1 teaspoon fine sea salt

About a dozen small new potatoes (7 ounces or 200 grams)

2 tablespoons olive oil, plus more for drizzling

1 pound (400 grams) fish (about 8 small mackerel fillets
    or 4 salmon steaks)

2 tablespoons chopped fresh chives

Freshly ground pepper

1 cup (50 grams) fresh breadcrumbs (you can use a food processor,
    or rub a thick slice of bread against the coarse side of
    a cheese grater)

1 large egg, lightly beaten

$\frac{1}{3}$ cup (40 grams) all-purpose flour

$\frac{1}{2}$ cup (40 grams) rolled oats

Preheat the oven to 425°F (220°C). Grease a large baking sheet.

(continued on next page)

Place the diced zucchini in a colander set over a bowl and sprinkle with the sea salt, tossing to coat. Set aside for 10 minutes to let the salt draw excess water out of the zucchini.

Finely dice the potatoes. Heat the olive oil in a large skillet over medium heat. Add the diced potatoes and sauté for 5 minutes, stirring occasionally to prevent sticking.

Shake the colander to drain off any water from the zucchini (the salt will act as a seasoning), then add to the skillet with the potatoes and sauté for another 5 minutes, until the zucchini are just slightly softened but not browned.

Skin and finely chop the fish, inspecting closely for bones, and place in a large mixing bowl. Add the cooked vegetables along with the chives, pepper, breadcrumbs, and egg. Stir thoroughly to combine.

Mix the flour and oats together in a shallow bowl.

Scoop up a handful of the fish mixture and squeeze hard between your palms to form a flattened cake. Dredge each side carefully in the flour mix and pop onto the prepared baking sheet. The mixture will be somewhat difficult to keep together, but the cakes will firm up and adhere during cooking. You should have sufficient mixture for 8 cakes. Drizzle some olive oil over the tops of the fish cakes and bake for 15 minutes, turning once halfway through cooking. The tops should be golden-brown and crisp at the edges.

Zucchini and Pesto Pizza

This is a totally green pizza without a tomato in sight: just paper-thin slices of simply juicy, sweet zucchini layered over a purée of aromatic basil and garlic. The quantities given are for one single-serving pizza—when do people ever agree on exactly the same combination of toppings? The secret to this pizza is really fresh zucchini, which ideally you could pick to order.

Makes one 10-inch pizza

1 zucchini (about 4 ounces or 100 grams)

1 tablespoon olive oil, plus more for drizzling

Coarse sea salt and freshly ground pepper

1 unbaked 10-inch thin Pizza Dough crust, rolled out

   (page 52)

1 tablespoon store-bought or homemade pesto, loosened with

   a splash of olive oil, if necessary

2 ounces (50 grams) fresh mozzarella, torn into pieces

Preheat the oven to 500°F (250°C).

   Using a vegetable peeler or mandolin, cut the zucchini lengthwise into paper-thin slices. Transfer the zucchini slices to a bowl and toss with the oil and salt and pepper to taste.

   Prepare the pizza on a sheet of flour-dusted cardboard or a thin cutting board so it can easily be slid onto a pizza stone or baking sheet.

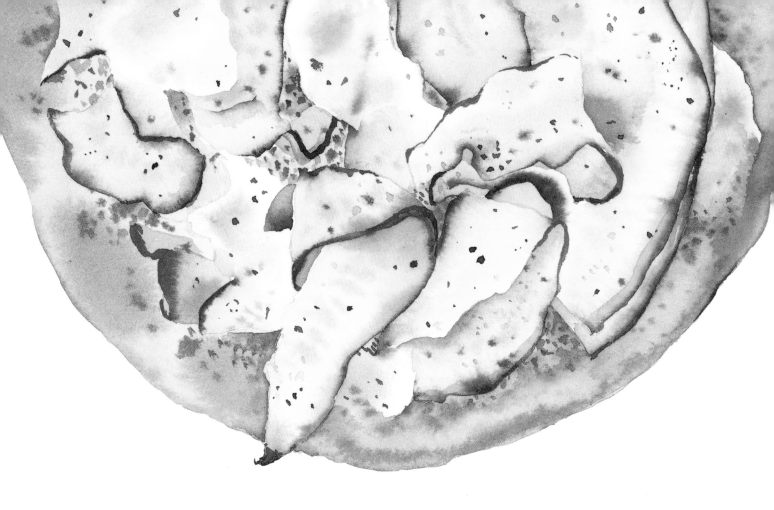

Spread the pesto sauce evenly over the pizza dough. Scatter the zucchini strips on top, then dot with the mozzarella. Add a quick, final drizzle of olive oil.

If you have a pizza stone, put it in the oven to heat through for 20 minutes before dusting with flour or cornmeal and sliding the topped pizza dough onto the stone. Alternatively, slide the pizza onto a perforated baking sheet or pizza pan, dusted with flour, and place in the oven.

Bake until the crust is golden and the toppings are bubbling, 7 to 10 minutes. If you need to bake pizzas in batches, make sure you have some warmed plates ready, then cover the pizzas loosely with foil.

Spinach and Egg Florentine Pizza

Featuring a classic combination of toppings, this pizza is one of my favorites and a must if you have your own fresh eggs. The egg looks stunning baked onto the center of the pizza.

Makes one 10-inch pizza

1 tablespoon olive oil, plus more for drizzling

2 cups (150 grams) chopped spinach or spinach beet (substitute ½ cup cooked or frozen)

1 unbaked 10-inch thin Pizza Dough crust, rolled out (page 52)

3 or 4 tablespoons Tomato Sauce (page 127)

1 very fresh egg

3 ounces (85 grams) fresh mozzarella, torn into pieces

6 oil-packed anchovy fillets

About a dozen good-quality pitted black olives, such as kalamata

Preheat the oven to 500°F (250°C).

Heat 1 tablespoon of olive oil in a small skillet over medium heat. Add the spinach and sauté for 4 minutes, tossing regularly until all the liquid has evaporated and the spinach is wilted. Season well with salt and pepper, and set aside.

Prepare the pizza on a sheet of flour-dusted cardboard or a thin cutting board so it can easily be slid onto the pizza stone or baking sheet.

Spread the tomato sauce evenly over the pizza dough. Squeeze any excess water from the spinach through a fine mesh sieve; scatter the spinach in little clumps over the sauce. Carefully crack the egg into the center of the pizza. Scatter the mozzarella over the pizza, avoiding the egg. Dot the anchovies and olives evenly over the top, and finish with a drizzle of olive oil.

If you have a pizza stone, put it in the oven to heat through for 20 minutes before dusting with flour or cornmeal and sliding the topped pizza dough onto the stone. Alternatively, slide the pizza onto a perforated baking sheet or pizza pan, dusted with flour, and place in the oven.

Bake until the crust is golden and the egg is set to your liking, 7 to 10 minutes. If you need to bake pizzas in batches, make sure you have some warmed plates ready, then cover the pizzas loosely with foil.

Pasta with Sugar Snap Peas and Salmon

The long, green pods and crunchy sweet flesh of sugar snap peas need minimal cooking. Tossed with pasta, over salmon, they make a quick and fresh supper dish. As the emphasis here is "quick," use fresh or dried tagliatelle, cooked according to package directions. A fresh green salad completes the meal.

Serves 4

¾ cup (200 milliliters) dry white wine

1 pound (400 grams) boneless skinless salmon fillet,

    portioned into 4 pieces if desired

1 pound (450 grams) dried pasta or 1¼ pounds (550 grams)

    fresh pasta

4 tablespoons olive oil, divided

12 ounces (300 grams) sugar snap peas, trimmed if necessary

3 tablespoons chopped fresh flat-leaf parsley

1½ cups (350 milliliters) heavy whipping cream (or double cream)

2 tablespoons freshly grated Parmesan cheese, plus more

    for sprinkling

Place a large lidded skillet over low heat and add the wine, allowing it to warm. When the wine just barely begins to bubble, add the salmon fillets in a single layer. Cover the pan and allow the fish to gently poach for about 10 minutes, until opaque.

Lift the salmon from the pan, reserving the wine, and flake into medium-size pieces into a bowl; cover to keep warm. Bring the reserved wine in the skillet to a boil; continue to boil rapidly until the wine is reduced by half.

42

Meanwhile, bring a large pot of salted water to boil. Cook the pasta according to package directions.

While the pasta is cooking, heat 2 tablespoons of olive oil in a medium skillet over medium heat. Add the peas and the parsley, and stir-fry for 2 to 3 minutes, tossing regularly with a spatula, until the peas are al dente. Add the cream and the reduced wine and simmer for about 1 minute, until heated through. Stir in the Parmesan and the salmon, and season with salt and pepper.

Drain the pasta thoroughly with drizzle with the remaining 2 tablespoons of olive oil. Add the sautéed vegetables with cream sauce and stir gently to combine.

Serve with extra Parmesan cheese for sprinkling.

Sugar Snap Peas

I have a row of sugar snap peas that were just a couple of inches tall all winter, sitting under a protective cloche. They have tolerated frost, snow, and ice, but now at four feet tall they are rejoicing in sunshine and warmth. The flowers are as beautiful as any sweet pea, deep magenta and fuchsia pink.

Posh B.L.T.s

As the title implies, these little sandwiches make luxurious lunch or picnic fare, and are sophisticated enough to be accompanied by a glass of sparkling wine. I first came across gougères in France: delicious, bite-size morsels of pâte à choux pastry baked with Parmesan and lardons are served warm with drinks. I sometimes embellish the freshly baked cheese puffs with added herbs, or stuff them with cream cheese. Gougères are best the day they're made, but can be kept overnight in an airtight container, or frozen and warmed in the oven.

Makes 8 to 10 small sandwiches

PÂTE À CHOUX

½ cup (115 grams) unsalted butter

1 cup (240 milliliters) water

¾ cup (100 grams) all-purpose flour

Pinch of salt

3 large eggs

3 tablespoons freshly grated Parmesan cheese

FILLING

10 very thin slices prosciutto

6 lettuce leaves, preferably something delicate and frilly,
    like Bibb (Boston) or oakleaf

5 small ripe tomatoes (about 12 ounces or 300 grams), sliced

Mayonnaise for serving (optional)

Preheat the oven to 400°F (200°C). Line a baking sheet with parchment paper.

Combine the butter and water in a heavy pot over medium-low heat. Cover and heat slowly, so that as the water is boiling the butter has melted. Remove the lid and with the water boiling rapidly, add the flour and salt and remove from the heat. Immediately beat the mixture vigorously with a wooden spoon until it becomes smooth and glossy and pulls cleanly away from the sides of the pot.

Transfer the dough to a large mixing bowl to cool for about 5 minutes (stirring the dough occasionally will speed up the process).

Whisk the eggs lightly with a fork, then beat them into the dough a little at a time with a wooden spoon. The mixture should be soft but not runny; it should easily drop off the spoon when tapped on the side of the bowl. You may not need to add all the egg. Stir in the Parmesan.

Drop heaping tablespoonfuls of dough onto the prepared baking sheet; there should be sufficient dough for 8 to 10 gougères. Bake for 10 minutes, then lower the heat to 350°F (180°C) and continue to bake for 30 minutes, until they are golden brown and puffy, and feel crisp. Don't be tempted to take them out of the oven too early as the middles will still be soggy and they may deflate.

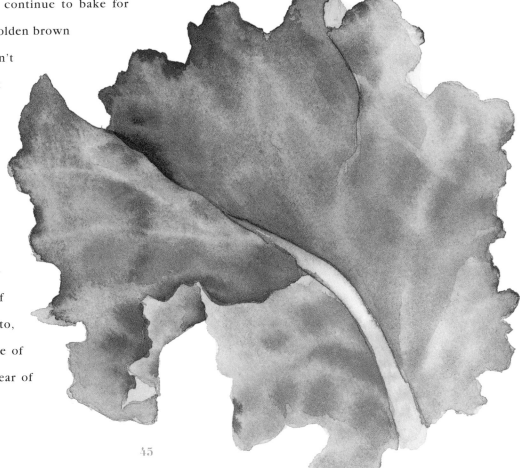

Transfer the baking sheet to a wire cooling rack. Let cool slightly, then slice each gougère horizontally. Fill each cheese puff with a slice of prosciutto, some torn lettuce, a couple of slices of tomato, and a smear of mayonnaise. Bon appètit!

Lamb Shanks with Red Wine and Raisins

Long, slow cooking makes the lamb beautifully tender, while tomatoes, raisins, and cinnamon steep in the red wine to make a rich, aromatic gravy. This is a perfect dish to serve with fresh spring vegetables; at this point in the year, the garden should at least be able to offer spinach beet, sprouting broccoli, cavolo nero, and spring cabbage! On a thrifty note, this recipe works equally well with turkey; your butcher may well have a stock of post-Thanksgiving drumsticks in his freezer. Spinach Mashed Potatoes with a Hint of Garlic (page 222) also makes a wonderful side.

Serves 4 generously

2 tablespoons olive oil

4 lamb shanks

2 garlic cloves

1 medium onion, diced

10 ounces (250 grams) fresh tomatoes (about 2 medium), peeled and quartered, or substitute canned peeled tomatoes

½ bottle (generous 1½ cups or 375 milliliters) dry red wine

2 teaspoons ground cinnamon

1 cup (150 grams) raisins

2 cups (500 milliliters) beef stock, plus more as needed

3 bay leaves

Fine sea salt and freshly ground pepper

Preheat oven to 325°F (165°C).

Heat the oil in a large skillet over medium-high heat. Add the lamb shanks and brown on all sides, in batches if necessary. Transfer the lamb to a large, lidded casserole, or rimmed baking dish that can be covered with foil.

In the same skillet over low heat, add a splash more oil if necessary and gently sauté the garlic and onion until soft. Add the tomatoes and simmer for 5 minutes. As the tomatoes soften, pick out any skins that come loose.

Add the red wine and the cinnamon, bring to a boil, and simmer for 5 minutes. Add the raisins, stock, and bay leaves; cook just to heat through, and season with salt and pepper.

Pour the contents of the skillet over the lamb shanks. Cover and cook in the oven for 3 hours, until the meat is falling off the bone. Check the liquid levels towards the end of the cooking time, adding more stock if necessary. Adjust seasonings to taste.

Baked Rhubarb

One of the simplest age-old methods of cooking rhubarb highlights the contrast of tart rhubarb flesh with sweet syrup. This must be served with something deliciously creamy like mascarpone or Greek yogurt, and Crisp Butter Biscuits (page 49).

Serves 4 to 6

1½ pounds (700 grams) rhubarb (about 6 or 7 stalks), the redder the better

Juice of 1 orange

6 whole cloves

¾ cup (150 grams) castor (superfine) sugar

A few curls of orange zest, for serving

. . . .

Preheat the oven to 300°F (150°C).

Cut the rhubarb into 3-inch lengths and spread in a single layer in a large rimmed baking dish. Pour the orange juice over the top, dot the cloves over evenly and sprinkle the sugar onto the rhubarb. Cover with a tight layer of foil and bake for 30 to 40 minutes, or until the rhubarb is completely soft but still retains its shape. Discard the cloves.

Allow rhubarb to cool to room temperature. Dish out a nice little pile of rhubarb logs in a puddle of syrup onto each plate, with a pinch of orange zest strewn over the top.

Crisp Butter Biscuits

These cookies have a lovely crunchy bite, and pair well with soft, fruity desserts. They are also good tools for stabbing into ice cream. A coarse cornmeal is important, so choose a gritty variety.

Makes 25 biscuits

1 tablespoon sunflower oil

¼ cup (40 grams) sliced almonds (optional)

½ teaspoon salt

½ cup (115 grams) unsalted butter, melted

½ cup (100 grams) castor (superfine) sugar

1 large egg

¾ cup (75 grams) all-purpose flour

⅓ cup (50 grams) polenta or coarse cornmeal

Preheat oven to 350°F (180°C).

Line a large baking sheet with parchment paper.

If you are including the nuts, heat the sunflower oil in a small skillet over medium-low heat. Add the almonds and salt and cook for 3 to 4 minutes, stirring frequently, until the almonds start to brown and smell toasty. Remove from the heat immediately to prevent from burning, and pour into a small bowl to cool.

With an electric mixer, whisk together the butter with the sugar and egg until pale and fluffy. Stir in the flour and polenta with a spoon until just combined, and stir in the toasted almonds.

Drop large teaspoonfuls about 2 inches apart on the prepared baking sheet and bake for 12 minutes, until the edges turn golden-brown. Remove from the oven and cool on the baking sheet for a couple of minutes before transferring to a wire rack to cool completely.

Pink Tea Party
Meringue-Cream Sandwiches

A splash of beet juice is usually an unwanted menace in the kitchen. But here, beet juice is put to good use: it's a lovely alternative to commercially prepared food coloring and won't impart any vegetable taste to the baked meringues. Meringues are best eaten fresh, but unfilled meringues will keep at room temperature in an airtight container for up to 4 days; sandwich them together with whipped cream just before serving.

Makes 1 dozen

2 large egg whites, at room temperature

Pinch fine sea salt

½ cup (100 grams) castor (superfine) sugar

½ teaspoon white vinegar

2 teaspoons beet juice (unseasoned baked beets will yield a puddle of juice; see page 78)

¾ cup (150 milliliters) heavy whipping cream

Preheat the oven to its lowest setting, about 225°F (110°C), or lower if possible. Line a baking sheet with parchment paper and lightly grease.

Combine the egg whites and salt in a scrupulously clean, dry bowl, free from any grease. Whisk with an electric mixer set on the highest speed for about a minute, until they hold stiff peaks.

Whisk in half the sugar, a little at a time, then fold in the remainder gradually with a spatula. Finally fold in the vinegar and beet juice.

Place evenly sized spoonfuls of meringue on the prepared baking sheet. If you keep to generous

teaspoonfuls, you should be able to make 24.

Bake for 2 hours, until they feel crisp to the touch. Turn the oven off, and allow the meringues to cool on the baking sheet inside.

When the meringues are cool, whip the cream with an electric mixer on medium speed until it forms stiff peaks. Sandwich the bases of the meringues together with a generous spoonful of whipped cream and serve immediately.

Pizza Dough

The best pizza I have ever tasted was, reassuringly and not surprisingly, in Italy many years ago. I don't think anyone quite forgets their first Italian pizza. The benchmark is set forevermore. I never have quite been able to recreate such an alluring combination of crispiness of crust, succulent mozzarella, sweet tomato, wilted spinach, and salty anchovy. The sun has never been quite so hot and I know for a fact that the Leaning Tower of Pisa doesn't lean as much as it did then! Traditionally, the pizza dough would be made the day before cooking, giving a long rising time, and resulting in a softer crust. When I have the time, this is a great technique. Most of the time, however, I make the dough quickly last thing at night, leave in a warm place to rise, then pop it in the fridge the next morning where it will keep for up to a week. All you have to worry about then is the toppings.

Makes 4 thin (10-inch) crusts

2 teaspoons active dry yeast

1 tablespoon castor (superfine) sugar

1 tablespoon olive oil

1¼ cups (300 milliliters) lukewarm water (110 to 115°F)

3½ cups (500 grams) unbleached white bread flour, plus more as needed

1 teaspoon fine sea salt

In a medium bowl, combine the yeast, sugar, oil, and water; stir well, then set aside until the yeast begins to froth, for 5 to 10 minutes. In a large mixing bowl, sift together the flour and salt. Make a well in the center of the flour and gradually pour the yeast mixture into the well, stirring as you go to incorporate all the flour. Once you have added all the water, use your hands to form the dough into a ball. Move the dough to a floured board and knead for 2 or 3 minutes, or until the dough is smooth and elastic without sticking to the board.

Put the dough in a lightly oiled bowl, cover with a damp cloth, and leave to rise in a warm place until doubled in bulk, about 1 hour, depending on the temperature and humidity. Punch the dough down, place it on the floured board, and briefly knead out the air.

Divide the dough into 3 or 4 equal-size pieces and stretch or roll out thinly. Add toppings of your choice, or try Spinach and Egg Florentine Pizza (page 40), or Zucchini and Pesto Pizza (page 38).

Preheat the oven to 500°F (250°C).

Prepare the pizza on a sheet of flour-dusted cardboard or a thin cutting board so they can easily be slid onto the pizza stone or baking sheet.

If you have a pizza stone, put it in the oven to heat through for 20 minutes before dusting with flour or cornmeal and sliding the topped pizza dough onto the stone. Alternatively, slide the pizza onto a perforated baking sheet or pizza pan, dusted with flour, and place in the oven.

Bake until the crust is golden and the toppings are bubbling, 7 to 10 minutes. If you need to bake pizzas in batches make sure you have some warmed plates ready for the finished pizzas, then cover them loosely with foil.

Basic Bread

While it's natural for most of us to be inspired by picking an armful of fresh produce from the garden, it's not necessarily so easy to get excited by a bag of flour and a jug of water. But that's precisely what I love about making bread: the cupboards can seem bare but within a couple of hours, you can be dipping warm balls of dough into garlic butter, eating fresh pizzas, or toasting currant loaf over the fire. It's comfort food at its most versatile! For everyday bread, I use half unbleached white bread flour and half whole wheat flour. In this recipe, I have used unbleached white bread flour for a dough that can be adapted for "fancy breads." See Herbed Focaccia on page 128 and Pear Walnut Focaccia on page 202 for more uses.

Makes 1 loaf

3 ¼ cups plus 2 tablesppons (450 grams) unbleached white bread flour

2 ¼ teaspoons (¼-ounce packet) active dry yeast

1 tablespoon castor (superfine) sugar

1 teaspoon fine sea salt

1 ½ cups (350 milliliters) lukewarm water

Grease a 10 x 5-inch loaf pan.

Measure the flour into a large mixing bowl and make a well in the center of the flour; add the yeast, sugar, and salt in the well. Gradually pour the water into the well, stirring until a soft dough forms. Turn the dough onto a floured board and knead for 2 to 3 minutes, until it feels smooth and elastic and does not stick to the board, adding more flour as necessary. The more you knead the lighter the texture of the bread will be. (I find, however, that spending just a few minutes making up a batch of dough while waiting for the kettle to boil rather than devoting a whole afternoon to the process means I'm much more likely to get around to it. Just keep it simple.) Return the dough to the large mixing bowl, cover with a damp cloth, and leave to rise in a warm place until doubled in bulk, about 1 to 2 hours, depending on the temperature and humidity.

Return the dough to the lightly floured board, knead for a few seconds to release the air, and shape into a fat sausage to fit into the loaf pan. Cover and leave in a warm place to rise again, this time for about half an hour, until the bread has risen slightly higher than the top of the pan.

Preheat the oven to 400°F (200°C).

Bake the bread for 25 minutes, or until the crust is quite firm and sounds hollow when tapped. Turn the loaf out of the pan immediately to keep the edges from becoming soggy. Cool the bread on a wire rack.

Mayonnaise

Mayonnaise is best made often and in small batches. It should only be kept, refrigerated, for 3 or 4 days because it contains raw egg, and should not be eaten by the very young, the very old, the infirm, or expectant mothers due to the slight risk of salmonella. If that hasn't put you off making it, you will be rewarded with a thick, creamy, zingy dressing quite different from anything bought in a store. You can vary the recipe each time you make it: add a little mustard, herbs, garlic, or lemon.

Makes 1¼ cups (300 milliliters)

2 egg yolks, at room temperature

1 tablespoon freshly squeezed lemon juice

1 cup (240 milliliters) grapeseed oil

½ teaspoon white wine vinegar

Fine sea salt and freshly ground pepper

Combine the egg yolks and the lemon juice in a deep bowl and beat with an electric mixer on high speed for a couple of minutes, until thick. Literally drop by drop, begin to add the oil, beating continuously. Once you have added about half of the oil and the mixture has started to thicken, you can then add the oil in a very, very thin trickle, still beating furiously. Once the mayonnaise is very thick, whisk in the vinegar and season to taste with salt and pepper.

Anchovy Mayonnaise

This salty mayonnaise is great as a dip when you just want to munch your way through a plateful of raw vegetables.

Serves 6 to 8

12 salt-packed anchovies, rinsed and drained

1¼ cups (300 milliliters) Mayonnaise (page 56)

. . . .

Finely chop the anchovies and combine them in a bowl with 1 tablespoon of the mayonnaise. Using a fork, mash the anchovies into the mayonnaise, and when thoroughly combined, add the remaining mayonnaise and mix thoroughly.

Honey-Mustard Vinaigrette

This very basic vinaigrette is a good one to have in the fridge. It can easily be tweaked to your taste by adding seasonal herbs or roasted garlic.

Makes about 1¼ cups (300 milliliters)

½ cup (120 milliliters) extra-virgin olive oil

2 tablespoons white wine vinegar

2 tablespoons freshly squeezed lemon juice

1 tablespoon Dijon mustard

4 teaspoons honey, warmed if necessary to drizzle easily

Fine sea salt and freshly ground pepper

Combine all the ingredients in a clean glass jar, screw the lid on tightly, and give it a good shake to blend. Alternatively, beat the ingredients together with a fork in a bowl. Adjust seasoning to taste. Keep in a lidded jar in the fridge for 2 to 3 weeks.

Rhubarb Curd

Once you have an established rhubarb plant in your garden there's not much to prevent it from bursting forth with succulent pink stems year after year. This bountiful garden resident can be transformed into delicious pies, puddings, sauces, and preserves right through to mid-summer. For the earliest possible rhubarb, place an upturned bucket over the crown to force the stems. They'll shoot up searching for light, way ahead of those in open ground. As soon as it's warm enough, dust down the garden furniture and sit outside for a seasonal afternoon tea of freshly made scones topped with pink rhubarb curd.

Makes three 8-ounce (300 gram) jars

1 ¼ pounds (500 grams) rhubarb (the younger and pinker the better), old green stems trimmed and discarded, coarsely chopped

½ cup (115 grams) unsalted butter

1 cup (225 grams) castor (superfine) sugar

2 large eggs

Combine the rhubarb, butter, and sugar in a nonreactive stainless steel saucepan (a reactive pan will impart a metallic taste) over low heat, and simmer for about 20 minutes, or until the rhubarb is soft. Let cool to room temperature.

Beat the eggs well to combine the yolks and whites, then quickly incorporate into the cooled rhubarb. Return the saucepan to the heat, and stirring continuously with a wooden spoon, cook on a very low heat for 10 minutes or so, until the mixture thickens. (If your stovetop does not have very sensitive controls, transfer the rhubarb custard to a double boiler. The egg will curdle if cooked too quickly.) Patience is the secret ingredient to a smooth curd.

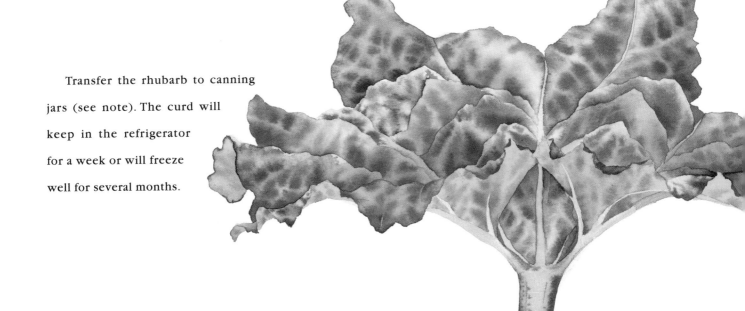

Transfer the rhubarb to canning jars (see note). The curd will keep in the refrigerator for a week or will freeze well for several months.

Sterilizing glass canning jars and bottles

Preheat the oven to 325°F (170°C). Wash the jars or bottles in hot soapy water, drain and lay on their side directly on the oven shelf. Leave in the oven for ten minutes, then remove carefully with oven gloves and fill while still warm.

Wash the lids in hot soapy water, but to be scrupulous, also submerge them in a pot of gently boiling water for ten minutes, remove with tongs, and dry with a clean cloth.

Fill the jars while the contents are still hot, and screw on the lids fingertip-tight.

Summer

"I value my garden more for being full of blackbirds than of cherries,
and very frankly give them fruit for their songs."

—Joseph Addison, 1672–1719

Summer is the season of bounty. There are

fat rows of lettuce and clustered blossoms on the tomatoes. The zucchini are picking

up speed and slender pods dangle from the bean poles. Revenge is sweet on the

nettles—the roots must be dug up and discarded, but I cut up the tops and steep them

in water for a few days to make a liquid fertilizer for the tomatoes. They're also great activators for

the compost heap, and the youngest tips make a delicious soup. Good thing we have so many of them!

The local roads are at their prettiest now. I have the perfect circular jogging route, and part of

the challenge is to discover something new on each run. The year starts demurely with white violets,

primroses, and cowslips. Then blackthorn and May blossoms erupt from the thickets and bounding

hares effortlessly outstrip my pace. By early summer the air is perfumed with wild roses and honey-

suckle, and mother duck shepherds a dozen fuzzy ducklings to water.

We're feasting on young broad beans from the garden that are so tender they cook in barely a minute,

and peas that seldom make it into the kitchen because they've been eaten en route. Lunch is a handful

of salad leaves with chopped scallions and roasted beets. The birds have eaten all the cherries—they

always do—but we have had enough strawberries and currants to fill the pantry with jam.

The Indian bean tree is the last to blossom, and in the summer heat it looks strangely snow-covered

under a dusting of white orchid-like, frilly-edged blooms. Its wide, sweeping branches overhanging the

pond are the perfect place for the hammock. Ah, the hammock! The perfect place to laze, watching for

a flash of azure from the resident kingfisher. I have never yet spotted the kingfisher and I very rarely

find time to dangle in the hammock.

Summer

Side Dishes and Starters

Tomato and Mozzarella Stacks

Runner Bean and Tomato Salad

Roasted Green and Yellow Beans

Salmon Ceviche with Green Beans

Bonfire Beets with Anchovy Dressing

Beet Mousse on Chive-Butter Crostini

Crunchy Summer Salad

Celery Root Salad

Cucumber Ribbon Salad

Summer Salad on French Toast

Shaved Zucchini with Feta

Swiss Chard with Peas

Summer Vegetable Soup with Twist of Lime Croutons

Herb Cake

Mains

Tagliatelle with Green and Yellow Beans and Fennel-Spiced Pork

Roasted Fish with Zucchini and Tomato

Pasta with Roasted Bell Peppers

Frittata with Gingered Peas and Shrimp

Halloumi and Eggplant Skewers

Tomato–Lime Couscous

Coconut Chicken with Green Beans

Creamy Spinach–and–Mushroom Lasagna

Desserts

Summer Fruit Puffs

Strawberry Meringues

Strawberry Sorbet

Strawberry Shortcake

Basic Ice Cream

Plum and Marzipan Ice Cream

Plum and Rhubarb Curd Tart

Real Fruit Gelatin Salad

Sundries

Tomato Sauce

Herbed Focaccia

Fresh Tomato and Basil Bread

Scallion Breadsticks

Chile Jam

Chile and Cream Cheese Dip

Pink Grapefruit Dressing

Roasted Garlic Vinaigrette

Elderflower Cordial

Elderflower Fizz

Strawberry and Elderflower Jam

Scones

Rhubarb and Ginger Jam

Tomato and Mozzarella Stacks

Tomatoes, basil, and mozzarella are very happy companions; combined overnight, their flavors become inseparable and extra-delicious. You will need four 4-ounce dariole or baba molds (small tins about 2 inches high used for round pastries, slightly wider at the opening than at the bottom), to make four individual molded stacks, which you will invert onto serving plates; you can substitute espresso cups for the molds. Alternatively, use a 1-pint dish and divide the stack into quarters for serving.

Serves 4

4 slices day-old bread

Olive oil

1 pound (450 grams) cherry tomatoes

Fine sea salt and freshly ground pepper

1 cup fresh basil leaves (about 25 grams)

2 (4-ounce or 125-gram) fresh mozzarella balls, cut into ¼-inch-thick slices

Balsamic vinegar, for serving (optional)

Edible flower petals, for serving (optional)

Using the dariole mold as a cutter, cut out a circle from each slice of bread to fit each mold. Reserve the scraps for another use or discard.

Line the molds with plastic wrap, leaving a good amount hanging over the outside, and brush the wrap with a little olive oil.

Chop each tomato into about 8 pieces and discard any loose seeds. Transfer the chopped tomatoes to a sieve set over a bowl to drain. Drain for 10 minutes, then discard any juice and place the tomatoes in the bowl. Drizzle with a tablespoon of olive oil, and season well with salt and pepper.

Place 1 basil leaf flat in the base of each mold, followed by a slice of mozzarella. Then sprinkle on a rounded tablespoon of chopped tomato to cover the mozzarella, and a couple of torn basil leaves. Repeat the process twice more, finishing with a layer of tomato.

Drizzle the circles of bread with olive oil, then use them to cover the final layer of tomato. Fold the plastic wrap over the bread and press the bread firmly into the layers. Put the molds in the refrigerator overnight, weighted with a cutting board or cans placed atop a pan to compress the layers.

Remove the molds from the fridge half an hour before serving. Invert onto 4 separate plates just before serving. They're great just as they are, or with a splash of balsamic vinegar on the plate if you like. Decorate with a scattering of edible petals such as borage, marigold, or viola, if desired.

Runner Bean and Tomato Salad

Blanched beans, broiled tomatoes, and a few vinegary capers unite in a salad that can be chilled or eaten at room temperature, and won't spoil quickly. Use young beans and very sweet tomatoes. If you think your tomatoes are not quite up to scratch, a little tip is to sprinkle them with a teaspoon of sugar when grilling.

Serves 4

4 ripe tomatoes (about 12 ounces or 300 grams)

2 tablespoons olive oil, plus more for drizzling

Fine sea salt and freshly ground pepper

8 ounces (250 grams) runner beans, cut on the diagonal
  into 3-inch lengths, or substitute green beans

1 teaspoon very small capers packed in brine, chopped
  if necessary

Balsamic vinegar, as needed

Preheat the broiler or grill to medium-high.

Cut the tomatoes into quarters and arrange on a rimmed baking sheet. Drizzle the tomatoes with the olive oil, sprinkle with salt and pepper, and cook under the broiler for 5 minutes, until tender but not completely collapsed.

Prepare an ice-water bath in a large bowl.

Fill a large saucepan with an inch of water; cover and bring to a boil over medium heat. Add the beans and cook for 2 to 3 minutes, until bright green and al dente. They should be just tender enough to pierce with the tip of a knife. Drain immediately and plunge the beans into the ice-water bath to stop the cooking completely. Transfer the beans to a kitchen towel to drain.

Combine the beans, tomatoes, and capers in a serving bowl, crushing the tomatoes a bit with a wooden spoon, and drizzle with a little olive oil and a few drops of balsamic vinegar to taste. Serve at room temperature, with a hot main dish, or chill.

Scarlet Runner Beans

All the runner beans I have seen for sale in the grocery store look ancient, dry, stringy, and sad! If for the same reason you have been put off buying them, try growing your own. Pick them young and fresh, eat them in season, and you will be converted. Mature pods become inedibly fibrous, but the fat purple or white seeds inside are delicious added to soups or casseroles. They are exceptionally easy to grow, have pretty scarlet, white, or lilac flowers, will tolerate some shade, and will supply you with beans all summer. A pot and some balcony railings will do fine.

Roasted Green and Yellow Beans

If you grow beans you will know the satisfaction of picking the pods daily, trying to keep pace with the crop. They are delicious roasted with scallions, and served warm as a side with pasta dishes or Caramelized Onion Dumplings (page 238).

Serves 4

12 ounces (300 grams) mixed green and yellow wax beans

3 scallions, cut into ¼-inch slices

1 ounce (30 grams) hazelnuts, coarsely chopped

2 tablespoons olive oil

Coarse sea salt and freshly ground pepper

Preheat the oven to 425°F (220°C).

Snap the stems off the beans. Cut the beans in half and place them in a large bowl. Add the scallions and the hazelnuts. Drizzle the olive oil over the vegetables, and toss well until evenly coated.

Spread the beans on a large baking sheet, season well with salt and pepper, and roast for 10 to 15 minutes, until tender and just beginning to brown. Turn with a spatula halfway through cooking.

Let the beans cool on the baking sheet slightly before serving.

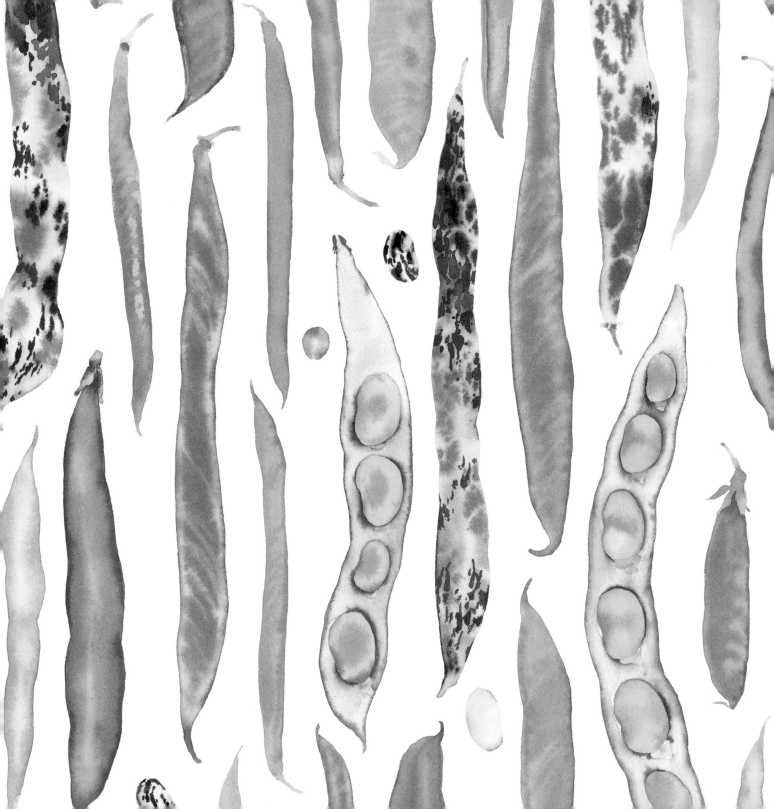

Salmon Ceviche with Green Beans

Roasted green beans with salmon marinated in pink grapefruit juice makes a sophisticated summer starter. The salmon should be very fresh, as it is not cooked, but steeped raw in citrus juices. (Your fishmonger should be able to recommend a salmon suitable for ceviche.) Allow about an hour for the fish to marinate.

Serves 4

8 ounces (200 grams) skinless salmon fillet

Juice of ½ pink grapefruit

Juice of ½ lime

4 tablespoons extra-virgin olive oil

1 teaspoon chopped fresh dill

1 tablespoon chopped fresh chives

12 ounces (300 grams) green beans, trimmed and left whole

Olive oil for drizzling

1 teaspoon castor (superfine) sugar, plus more to taste

Fine sea salt and freshly ground pepper

Sliced whole wheat bread, for serving

Cut the salmon across the grain into very thin slices, about ⅛-inch thick. Place in a shallow dish. To make the marinade, combine the grapefruit and lime juices, olive oil, dill, and chives in a clean empty glass jar with a tight-fitting lid. Screw on the lid and shake well to blend.

Pour the marinade over the salmon; cover and leave in the fridge to marinate for 30 minutes to 1 hour. The fish will turn opaque when it is "cooked."

Prepare an ice-water bath in a large bowl. Fill a large pot with 1 inch of water. Place a steamer insert in the pot and bring the water to a boil over high heat. Alternatively, bring a large pot of water to a boil. Steam or boil the beans for about 3 minutes, until they are just al dente. Immediately transfer the beans to the ice bath for a few minutes to cool completely and stop the cooking, then drain well and place on a kitchen towel to dry.

Preheat the broiler on high.

Transfer the beans to a rimmed baking sheet, drizzle with olive oil, and season with salt and pepper. Toss to coat evenly. Broil the beans for about 3 minutes, or until they look toasted. Divide the beans among four plates in neat piles while still warm.

When the salmon is ready, drain it, reserving the marinade, and divide among 4 plates atop the beans. Stir the sugar into the grapefruit marinade, taste and add a little more sugar or salt and pepper if necessary, then drizzle a tablespoonful over each serving.

Serve with slices of whole wheat bread.

Bonfire Beets with Anchovy Dressing

The dense flesh of a beet can be baked slowly in a conventional oven, but when we have a bonfire smoldering for a few days, it seems the perfect opportunity to take advantage of its heat.

Serves 4

ROASTED BEETS

4 to 5 beets of roughly equal size (about 1 pound or 450 grams)

2 tablespoons olive oil

3 garlic cloves, crushed under the flat of a knife blade

3 or 4 sprigs of fresh rosemary

Coarse sea salt and freshly ground pepper

ANCHOVY DRESSING

2 tablespoons Greek-style yogurt

2 tablespoons crème fraîche

6 anchovy fillets, finely chopped

....

For the beets: Light the bonfire! Alternatively, preheat the oven to 375°F (190°C).

Wash and dry the beets well, leaving the roots intact and twisting off the leaves while taking care not to damage the skins. Place the beets on a double layer of heavy-duty aluminum foil, large enough to wrap them securely in a package.

Drizzle the beets with the olive oil, and scatter the garlic, rosemary, and salt and pepper to taste over them. Wrap the foil tightly around the beets and pop the package into the hot embers of the bonfire, remembering its location! Leave for about 1 ½ hours, until the beets are soft when pierced with a sharp knife. Alternatively, bake for about an hour in the oven, or until the beets are easily pierced with a sharp knife. Remove the foil package and vent to release steam.

For the dressing: Mix together the Greek yogurt and crème fraîche. Stir in the anchovies.

When cool enough to handle, rub the skins off the beets and chop the beets into large chunks. Serve warm or at room temperature with the dressing on the side for dipping.

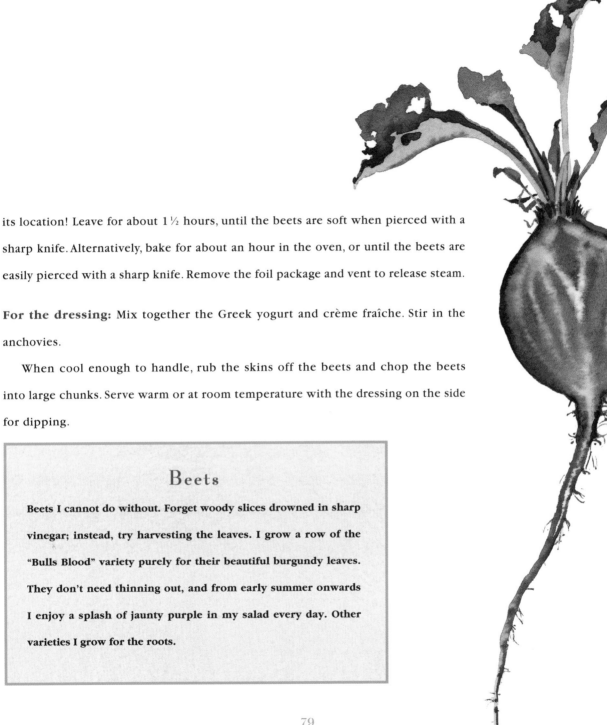

Beets

Beets I cannot do without. Forget woody slices drowned in sharp vinegar; instead, try harvesting the leaves. I grow a row of the "Bulls Blood" variety purely for their beautiful burgundy leaves. They don't need thinning out, and from early summer onwards I enjoy a splash of jaunty purple in my salad every day. Other varieties I grow for the roots.

Beet Mousse on Chive-Butter Crostini

I often eat my working lunch outside on a favorite bench. Day lilies brush my shoulders and sunflowers and holly-hocks tower overhead. If I could capture that sensation on a plate, beet mousse would be it. The vibrant color alone is a good enough reason to give this a try. Remember to make well in advance to allow time (3 to 4 hours) for the mousse to set up in the fridge. Sheets of gelatin are easy to use; with no danger of lumps, they dissolve immediately in hot liquids after being soaked in cold water. One sheet will set ½ cup of liquid. If sheet gelatin is unavailable, use a quantity of powdered gelatin to set 1 cup, according to package directions.

Serves 4

MOUSSE

2 sheets gelatin

½ cup (100 grams) cooked and chopped beets (see page 78)

5 tablespoons (100 grams) low-fat fromage frais or plain Greek-style yogurt

6 tablespoons (100 milliliters) heavy whipping cream

Fine sea salt and freshly ground pink peppercorns, or very finely ground black pepper

CROSTINI

1½ tablespoons unsalted butter, at room temperature

1 tablespoon chopped fresh chives, plus more for sprinkling

4 thick slices good-quality ciabatta bread

4 slices fresh mozzarella

For the mousse: Soak the gelatin sheets in cold water until soft, for about 5 minutes.

Combine the beets and fromage frais in a food processor or blender and whiz to a smooth paste, 1 to 2 minutes. Transfer to a bowl.

In a small heavy saucepan, heat the cream to just below boiling, remove from the heat, and add the gelatin sheets one at a time, whisking to ensure they are dissolved. Allow the cream to cool to room temperature.

Add the cooled cream to the beet paste and mix with a spoon until thoroughly combined. Season with salt and pepper to taste and transfer to a small serving dish, smoothing the paste evenly. Refrigerate for at least 3 to 4 hours to set.

For the crostini: In a small bowl, stir the chives into the softened butter to combine. Cover and set aside until ready to serve.

Just before serving, spread the ciabatta slices with the chive butter and grill or broil both sides until sizzling. Place a piece of mozzarella on each slice, then top with a spoonful of mousse and a final sprinkling of bright green chives.

Crunchy Summer Salad

Less cooking and more tossing together suits summer vegetables that are so sweet and tender they can be enjoyed raw, at least while they're very young. Don't leave this one sitting around for too long or the turnips will begin to go limp.

Serves 4

6 ounces (150 grams) sugar snap peas

6 small turnips (about 6 ounces or 150 grams), scrubbed well

6 small carrots (about 6 ounces or 150 grams), peeled

2 handfuls young beet leaves or baby spinach,
    washed and dried

Juice of 1 lime

1 tablespoon honey

2 tablespoons olive oil

A few fresh mint leaves, torn into small pieces, for serving

. . . .

Prepare an ice-water bath in a large bowl.

Fill a pot with 1 inch of water. Place a steamer insert in the pot and bring the water to a boil. Alternatively, bring a pot of water to a boil. Steam or boil the peas for 2 minutes, then plunge immediately into the ice-water bath until completely cool to stop the cooking. Transfer peas to a kitchen towel to drain.

Thinly slice the turnip. Halve the carrots lengthwise and cut into matchsticks. Tear the beet leaves into bite-size pieces, if necessary.

Combine the vegetables in a large bowl and toss together.

In a small bowl, combine the lime juice, honey, and olive oil. Whisk well with a fork to combine, then pour over the salad and toss well. Transfer to a pretty serving bowl and sprinkle with torn mint leaves.

Celery Root Salad

Possibly the best way to eat raw celery root, this salad is based on a classic French rémoulade: matchstick-thin strips of the root bathed in a mustardy mayonnaise. Before I even knew of celery root, I would gorge myself on this very common salad on holidays in France. Choose a small root which feels heavy and solid; larger roots and those that have been stored for too long have a tendency to be pithy inside, which is no good for this salad. Team it with salad greens.

Serves 4 to 6

1 celery root (about ¾ pound or 300 grams), peeled

Juice of 1 lemon

1 tablespoon sesame seeds (optional)

½ cup (120 milliliters) mayonnaise

1 tablespoon Dijon mustard

1 tablespoon chopped fresh flat-leaf parsley

Quarter the celery root, then cut into very thin, almost translucent slices, about ⅛-inch. Stack the slices and cut on the long end into thin matchsticks. Alternatively, use a julienne disc on a food processor. Be sure not to turn the root into a grated mush.

Transfer the chopped celery root to a bowl and toss with the lemon juice to keep it from turning brown and to soften it slightly. Cover and refrigerate for 30 minutes.

Spread the sesame seeds (if using) in a small dry skillet over medium heat and toast for 2 to 3 minutes, until just golden-brown and aromatic. Transfer sesame seeds to a small bowl and set aside.

Mix together the mayonnaise and the mustard; add to the celery root and combine thoroughly. Sprinkle with the sesame seeds and parsley, and serve.

Cucumber Ribbon Salad

This is a refreshing green salad with thin ribbons of cucumber and lettuce tossed in a creamy dressing. I prefer it made with a soft-leaved lettuce, such as green oak leaf or butterhead, but I use whatever needs picking. The salad should be put together just before serving or the cucumber will begin to wilt. You can make the dressing earlier in the day. To toast the pine nuts, preheat the oven to 350°F (180°F) and toast on a baking sheet for 5 minutes until fragrant and light golden, watching them carefully.

Serves 4 to 6

1 cucumber (approximately 12 inches or 30 centimeters), peeled if desired

½ head tender lettuce (about 6 ounces or 150 grams), washed and dried

2 tablespoons pine nuts, toasted

4 tablespoons olive oil

4 tablespoons low-fat plain Greek-style yogurt

2 tablespoons mayonnaise

6 fresh lemon balm or mint leaves, coarsely chopped or torn into small pieces

Fine sea salt and freshly ground pepper

Using a vegetable peeler or mandolin slicer, shave the cucumber with into thin strips about 6 inches long. Tear the lettuce leaves into manageable pieces. Toss both together in a large bowl.

Combine the olive oil, yogurt, mayonnaise, lemon balm, and salt and pepper to taste in a bowl and whisk with a fork until fully combined.

Just before serving, pour the dressing over the salad, toss, and transfer to a serving bowl. Scatter the toasted pine nuts over the top.

Summer Salad on French Toast

This is a quick lunchtime dish for a day when you think there isn't any food in the pantry. As long as there are a couple of slightly stale slices of bread in the bread bin and a fresh egg in the chicken coop (or egg carton), you'll not go hungry.

Serves 2

2 large eggs

½ cup (100 milliliters) whole milk

Generous pinch of smoked paprika

Fine sea salt and freshly ground pepper

2 slices of day-old bread, each cut in half if the loaf

    is wide

2 tablespoons butter

3 small carrots (about 3 ounces or 75 grams)

¼ bulb medium fennel (about 3 ounces or 75 grams)

¼ medium cucumber (about 3 ounces or 75 grams)

½ red bell pepper (about 3 ounces or 75 grams)

Honey–Mustard Vinaigrette (page 59) or another dressing

    of your choice

4 slices bacon (optional)

Preheat the oven to 375°F (190°C). Grease a rimmed baking sheet.

Crack the eggs into a wide bowl and beat with a fork. Add the milk, season with paprika, salt, and pepper, and whisk again to incorporate.

Submerge the sliced bread in the egg mix, let it sit for a few seconds, then turn the slices over. They should soak up all the egg.

Heat the butter in a large skillet over medium heat. When it begins to foam, add the sliced bread and cook for 2 to 3 minutes on each side, until it is lightly golden. Transfer to the baking sheet, reserving the skillet for the bacon (if using), and cook in the oven for about 10 minutes, turning once halfway through

cooking, until the toasts are a deep golden-brown and sizzling.

Meanwhile, using a vegetable peeler or a mandolin, shave the carrots, fennel, cucumber, and bell pepper into paper-thin slices. Toss them together in a bowl and drizzle, but not drown, with a little dressing. Set aside.

Place the skillet back on a medium heat, add the bacon, and fry for about 4 or 5 minutes, turning once, until crispy. Transfer the bacon to a cutting board and chop finely.

Place each toast on a warmed plate and top with a relaxed heap of salad. Scatter with the crispy shreds of bacon. Consume with greed!

Shaved Zucchini with Feta

With the zucchini just lightly cooked then doused in oil and feta, this becomes a deliciously creamy dish, which is good with chicken or pork. Alternatively, this could be served as a salad: leave the zucchini shavings uncooked, and let them marinate in the feta paste for 20 minutes.

Serves 4

4 zucchini (about 1 pound or 450 grams)

Juice of 1 lemon

1 teaspoon honey

4 tablespoons olive oil

5 ounces (140 grams) feta cheese

2 teaspoons fresh thyme leaves or 1 teaspoon dried

3½ tablespoons butter

Slice off the stem and tail ends of the zucchini and discard. Using a vegetable peeler or a mandolin, shave the zucchini into long thin strips. Transfer the strips to a colander to drain for 10 minutes.

In a small bowl, mix together the lemon juice, honey, and

olive oil with a fork until it is smooth and thick. Crumble in the feta and thyme and mix briefly to yield a lumpy paste.

Heat the butter in a large skillet over medium heat until foaming. Add the zucchini and cook, stirring with a spatula, for about 2 minutes, until al dente. Quickly stir in the feta paste, and transfer to a warmed serving dish.

Zucchini

Like an actor who can bring to life a multitude of characters, zucchini lends itself to many different roles.

You can prepare zucchini in 101 different ways: diced, sliced, grated, and whole. And a good thing, too, because you will likely be forced into such ingenuity by this summer squash's relentless production!

Wanting to try three or four new varieties this year, I may have planted too many, but my resolve is to pick them small. We'll see who wins!

Swiss Chard with Peas

Swiss chard has beautiful thick crunchy stems that retain a juicy bite when cooked, whereas the leaves become velvety. Throw in some peas as well and you get lovely bursts of sweetness tucked between the wilted leaves. Anchovy Mayonnaise (page 57) served alongside adds a salty and creamy contrast.

Serves 4

1 pound (450 grams) Swiss chard

1 tablespoon butter

1 garlic clove, thinly sliced

8 ounces (200 grams) shelled fresh peas (allow double weight for unshelled) or substitute frozen thawed peas

Fine sea salt and freshly ground pepper

Cut the stems off the chard and slice them into 3-inch lengths. Fill a large pot with 1 inch of water and bring it to a boil. Add the chard stems and simmer for 5 minutes, until they can be easily pierced with the tip of a knife. Drain well.

Slice the leaves into 1-inch-wide ribbons. Melt the butter in a large skillet over medium-low heat. Add the garlic and the Swiss chard leaves with a tablespoon of water; cover and cook for 2 to 3 minutes, or until the chard is bright green and tender. Add the parboiled stems and the peas and stir to combine, adding a splash more water if necessary. Cover and continue to cook for 2 to 3 minutes, until the peas are tender. Season with salt and pepper and serve warm.

Summer Vegetable Soup with Twist of Lime Croutons

There's a point in the year, somewhere between digging up the last of the root vegetables and picking the first tender salad leaves, when I shun soup in favor of salad for lunch. I first made this soup, however, when we were teetering on the edge of summer; the salad switch had occurred some time before. Warm and comforting, this is a mildly creamy soup studded with fresh peas, beans, and zucchini, and topped with brilliantly zesty lime croutons. If you don't have a lime, use a lemon to season the brilliantly zesty croutons, but whatever you do, don't let apathy tempt you not to make them; they're essential!

Serves 4

CROUTONS

2 thick slices good-quality white bread, cut into ½-inch chunks

Juice of 1 lime

2 tablespoons olive oil

SOUP

6 scallions (white and unwilted green parts), finely chopped

12 ounces (300 grams) new potatoes (about 15), peeled and cut into ¼-inch dice

2 small zucchini (about 8 ounces or 225 grams), cut into ¼-inch dice

2 tablespoons all-purpose flour

2 tablespoons olive oil

8 ounces (200 grams) green beans, trimmed and cut into 1-inch lengths

6 ounces (160 grams) shelled peas or young broad beans (allow double the weight with shells)

4 cups (900 milliliters) chicken or vegetable stock

2 tablespoons chopped fresh parsley

2 tablespoons chopped fresh marjoram

½ cup (100 milliliters) heavy whipping cream or low-fat crème fraîche

Fine sea salt and freshly ground pepper

For the croutons: In a medium bowl, combine the bread chunks with the lime juice and olive oil; toss to coat. Set a small skillet over low heat and cook the croutons, stirring frequently to avoid sticking, about 5 minutes, or until they have toasty, golden edges. Set aside.

Fill a pot with 1 inch of water. Place a steamer insert in the pot and bring the water to a boil. Steam the green beans and peas for 2 minutes, or until just al dente.

For the soup: Combine the scallions, potatoes, and zucchini in a bowl. Add the flour and toss to coat.

Heat the olive oil in a skillet over low heat. Add the flour-coated vegetables and sauté for 5 minutes, stirring regularly with a spatula to prevent sticking. Set aside in the skillet.

Meanwhile, bring the stock to a simmer in a large pot over medium-low heat; add all the cooked vegetables and the herbs. Simmer gently for about 6 minutes, or until the potato chunks are cooked through. Add the cream and heat through, then season to taste with salt and pepper.

Serve the soup in warmed bowls topped with the all-important croutons.

Herb Cake

By early summer, the garden is brimming with fragrant, soft-leaved herbs. This recipe captures that special bouquet in one soft, buttery mouthful. While rather generous in the fat content, this cross between bread and cake needs no embellishments other than a warm evening and a chilled glass of wine.

Makes 1 loaf

3 large eggs

¾ cup (170 grams) unsalted butter, melted

7 tablespoons (100 milliliters) whole milk

1¾ cups (180 grams) all-purpose flour

2 teaspoons baking powder

6 tablespoons chopped fresh soft-leaved herbs (parsley, chives, marjoram, or whatever you have on hand)

Fine sea salt and freshly ground pepper

. . . .

Preheat oven to 350°F (180°C).

Lightly grease an 8 x 4-inch loaf pan.

Using an electric mixer, beat the eggs until pale and frothy, then whisk in the melted butter and milk. Sift together the flour and the baking powder. Carefully add the sifted dry ingredients a little at a time until incorporated, stirring as little as possible. Add the herbs, season with salt and pepper, and pour into the prepared loaf pan.

Bake until the top is firm to the touch and a skewer inserted into the center comes out clean, about 30 minutes. Cool on a wire rack. Serve while still warm as a nibble with drinks.

Tagliatelle with Green and Yellow Beans and Fennel-Spiced Pork

If you can't find yellow wax beans, double up on the green. The combination with pasta and fennel-spiced pork reminds me of the deliciously aromatic porchetta stalls, obligatory in every Italian market, that tantalize hungry shoppers with warm, spit-roasted pork, stuffed with garlic and herbs.

Serves 4

PASTA DOUGH, or substitute 14 ounces (400 grams) dried tagliatelle

3 cups (300 grams) all purpose flour

Pinch sea salt

3 large eggs

PORK BALLS

2 teaspoons fennel seeds

1 pound (450 grams) ground pork

Fine sea salt and freshly ground pepper

1 tablespoon olive oil

1 recipe Tomato Sauce (page 127)

8 ounces (200 grams) yellow wax beans, stemmed and cut in half

8 ounces (200 grams) green beans, stemmed and cut in half

Freshly grated Parmesan cheese, for sprinkling

Handful of fresh basil, for serving

For the pasta: Stir together the flour and salt in a large mixing bowl. Make a well in the center of the flour mixture and crack the eggs into it. Start beating the egg into the flour with a fork. When nearly all the flour is incorporated, use your hands to form it into a ball of dough.

Flour a board and knead the dough vigorously for about five minutes, until it is silky and smooth. Pop the dough in a plastic bag and put it in the fridge to rest for half an hour.

Divide the pasta dough into 4 equal pieces. Divide each quarter into walnut-sized pieces, about 1¼-inches square. On a floured board, roll each small cube into a very thin sheet, about 4 x 8 inches. Lay them on clean kitchen towels to dry for 30 minutes, or until they are just pliable enough to roll up for cutting. Lay 6 sheets on top of one another, then start from the shortest edge and roll up, as you would a carpet. Slice the pasta into ¼-inch-thick strips, and unroll them as you place them in a large bowl. Repeat with the remaining sheets.

For the pork: Set a small dry skillet over medium heat and add the fennel seeds. Toast for 2 to 3 minutes, until they are aromatic and start to pop. Pour them into a mortar and use a pestle to grind them into a powder.

Place the pork in a bowl; add the ground fennel, salt, and pepper to season, and mix with a fork until thoroughly combined. Using your hands, shape the pork into small balls about the size of a walnut.

Heat the oil in a large skillet and fry the pork balls for 2 to 3 minutes, until brown on all sides, working in batches if necessary.

Bring the tomato sauce to a simmer in a large saucepan, then add the pork balls and simmer on low heat for 10 minutes.

Meanwhile, set a large pot of salted water for the pasta over high heat, and a smaller pot of water with a steamer insert, also over high heat, for the beans. Steam or boil the beans until al dente. When the pasta water is boiling rapidly, add the pasta and cook for 3 to 4 minutes at a rolling boil, until al dente. Test frequently to avoid overcooking. If using dried pasta, follow the package instructions.

Drain the pasta and the beans, returning both to the pasta pan, and add the tomato sauce and pork balls. Stir to combine.

Serve immediately in warmed shallow bowls. Sprinkle with Parmesan and festoon with some torn basil leaves.

Roasted Fish with Zucchini and Tomato

Perfectly roasted fish with a succulent topping of roasted tomato and zucchini is an easy dish to prepare, and can be adapted for serving with an impressive whole side of fish for a summer lunch party. Try substituting eggplant or red bell pepper for the zucchini. Serve with new potatoes and a selection of lightly steamed beans.

Serves 4

1 tablespoon olive oil, plus more for drizzling

2 small zucchini (about 10 ounces or 300 grams), cut into ¼-inch dice

12 salt-packed anchovies, rinsed and drained

1 tablespoon capers, packed in brine

Freshly ground pepper

12 sweet cherry tomatoes (about 4 ounces or 120 grams), finely diced

4 thick skinless fish fillets (cod, haddock, and salmon all work nicely), about 1¼ pounds (600 grams) total

. . . .

Preheat the oven to 400°F (200°C).

Heat the olive oil in a small skillet over medium-low heat. Add the zucchini and sauté gently for 3 to 4 minutes, until just soft. Towards the end of the cooking, add the anchovies and capers, and season with pepper. Transfer to a bowl and stir in the diced tomatoes.

Lay the fish fillets in a lightly oiled baking dish. Top each fillet with a scoop of the tomato-zucchini mixture, pressing firmly to help it adhere. Drizzle with a little olive oil and bake for 10 to 12 minutes, until the fish are just done and look opaque. Baking time will vary with thickness.

Pasta with Roasted Bell Peppers

This is a simple dish highlighting the silky, sweet flesh of roasted peppers. It's a good dish to serve on its own or as a *primi piatti*, followed by some grilled fish and vegetables.

Serves 4 to 6

2 large red bell peppers

6 tablespoons olive oil, divided, plus more for drizzling

1 pound dried spaghetti or another similar pasta

1 teaspoon chile oil or 1 teaspoon chopped red chile

4 garlic cloves, thinly sliced

½ cup (25 grams) fresh basil leaves, torn into pieces

¼ cup (30 grams) freshly grated Parmesan cheese, for sprinkling

Preheat the broiler to medium-high.

Quarter the peppers and remove the seeds and ribs. Place them in a bowl and drizzle with 2 tablespoons olive oil, tossing to coat evenly. Arrange the peppers on a rimmed baking sheet flesh-side up and broil for about 15 minutes, turning regularly, until tender and the skins blister and blacken slightly.

Transfer peppers to a bowl and cover with plastic wrap to sweat for 5 minutes. When cool enough to handle, peel off the skins, which should come off easily, but don't worry about every last scrap. Slice the flesh into ½-inch strips.

Bring a large pot of salted water to boil over high heat. Add the pasta and cook for 10 to 12 minutes, or until al dente. Drain and return to the pot, reserving a ladleful of pasta water.

While the pasta is cooking, heat the remaining 4 tablespoons olive oil and a teaspoon of chile oil in a large skillet over medium-low heat. Add the sliced garlic and sauté gently until softened. Add the ladleful of pasta water, the pepper strips, and the basil. Heat through, then add the cooked pasta and toss gently. Serve immediately sprinkled with Parmesan and drizzled with a little olive oil.

Frittata with Gingered Peas and Shrimp

Thanks to a steady supply of eggs from our chickens, frittata has become a real standby in our house. It is an easy dish which can be prepared with a variety of vegetables. Here, the deep-yellow eggs are studded with the sweetest of young peas, perfect for a light lunch accompanied by a salad. If you want to use frozen peas, try to find petits pois. Cut into small squares, this also serves as a nice hors d'oeuvre to accompany pre-dinner drinks.

Serves 4

2 tablespoons olive oil

1-inch piece fresh ginger, peeled and minced

1 cup (150 grams) shelled peas, preferably fresh, but frozen
   will work, too

6 large eggs

10 ounces (250 grams) uncooked peeled shrimp

2 tablespoons chopped fresh flat-leaf parsley

Fine sea salt and freshly ground pepper

2 tablespoons butter

Lemon wedges, for serving

Mayonnaise or plain yogurt, for serving

Preheat oven to 425°F (220°C).

Heat the olive oil in an oven-proof skillet over medium heat. Add the ginger and sauté until soft. Add the peas. If they are young and delicate, just toss them around in the oil for a few seconds; if they seem a bit tougher, add enough water to just cover, and simmer for 4 to 5 minutes until tender to the bite. Drain off any excess water, transfer the peas to a plate, and return the skillet to the heat.

Break the eggs into a bowl, whisk with a fork to lightly beat. Add the shrimp and parsley, and season with salt and pepper. Fold in the peas and ginger.

Melt the butter in the skillet and when it begins to foam, pour in the egg mixture, shuffling the shrimp around with a spoon to evenly distribute. Cook slowly over medium heat, stirring frequently but gently with a wooden spoon, as you would for scrambled eggs. When the egg is beginning to set but remains a bit runny on top, pop it into a hot oven and bake until the top is golden brown and puffy, 4 to 5 minutes. Check frequently and don't overcook; the eggs will carry on cooking from the heat of the pan once removed from the oven.

Slide the frittata onto a serving plate, let it cool slightly, then cut into thick slices. Enjoy with a green salad, a dollop of mayonnaise, and a good wedge of lemon to squeeze over it.

Halloumi and Eggplant Skewers

Halloumi, a delightful cheese originating on the Mediterranean island of Cyprus, seems most unassuming when you're preparing it for the first time: pallid, dense, salty, and that's about it. Roasted in the oven, however, it transforms with a crisp, squeaky exterior and soft, rich interior. Look for halloumi at better cheese shops and specialty food stores. Creamy eggplant serves to mop up the salty juices and cherry tomatoes add a sweet, fruity bite. Try these with Tomato-Lime Couscous (page 106) and a juicy Cucumber Ribbon Salad (page 85) on the side.

Makes eight 10-inch skewers

1 eggplant (about 1 pound or 450 grams), cut into
   1-inch cubes (about 32 cubes total)

Sea salt

4 tablespoons (25 grams) all-purpose flour

2 teaspoons paprika

Freshly ground pepper

1 pound (450 grams) halloumi cheese, cut into 32 cubes,
   about the same size as the eggplant cubes

32 cherry tomatoes (about 12 ounces or 300 grams)

4 tablespoons olive oil

If using wooden skewers, soak them in water for 30 minutes before cooking, to prevent them from burning. Preheat the oven to 400°F (200°C).

Put the eggplant in a colander set over a bowl. Sprinkle liberally with salt and leave to drain for 30 minutes. Rinse off the salt and pat the eggplant dry with a kitchen towel.

In a large bowl, combine the flour, paprika, and a twist of ground pepper. Add the halloumi cubes and toss gently. Transfer the cheese to another bowl and set aside. Add the eggplant to the remaining flour mixture and toss to coat.

Thread the halloumi, eggplant, and tomatoes onto the skewers, alternating to fit 4 pieces of each per skewer.

Arrange them carefully on a lightly greased rimmed baking sheet, drizzle with the olive oil, then roast in the oven for 15 minutes, turning halfway through cooking, until the halloumi is crisp and golden on the outside, the eggplant has begun to collapse slightly, and the tomatoes are beginning to burst their skins. Don't worry if bits and pieces fall off the skewers.

To serve, pull the skewers out at the table and serve hot.

Tomato-Lime Couscous

All the liquid added to the couscous is soaked up by the tiny pearls, so the lime juice, olive oil, and tomato juice give a real depth of flavor to this zesty side.

Serves 4

8 ounces (200 grams) quick-cooking couscous

Juice of 2 limes

¾ cup (200 milliliters) vegetable stock

4 tablespoons extra-virgin olive oil

4 tomatoes, chopped (about 1¾ cups or 280 grams)

4 tablespoons chopped fresh flat-leaf parsley

Fresh sea salt and freshly ground pepper

Put the couscous in a mixing bowl. Heat the lime juice and stock in a small saucepan to just below boiling. Alternatively, combine them in a microwave-safe dish and heat until it just boils. Add the olive oil, whisk with a fork, then pour the liquid over the couscous, stirring briefly to incorporate. Cover and leave to absorb for 10 minutes, then fluff up with a fork.

Stir in the chopped tomatoes and parsley along with any remaining juices, and season with salt and pepper to taste.

Coconut Chicken with Green Beans

The chile and ginger in this mildly spicy dish is just enough to balance the lovely nutty flavor of young green beans. Accompany this with basmati rice.

Serves 4

2 tablespoons sunflower oil or light olive oil

2 medium-to-hot fresh green chiles, finely chopped (jalapeño or Anaheim will work, or use whatever green chiles are available in your region)

2-inch piece fresh ginger, peeled and thinly sliced

2 garlic cloves, thinly sliced

4 skinless boneless chicken breast fillets, cut on the diagonal into ½-inch-thick strips

1¾ cups (400 milliliters) chicken stock, heated and kept warm

8 ounces (200 grams) green beans, stemmed and cut in half

½ cup (120 milliliters) good-quality coconut milk

Handful chopped fresh cilantro (coriander), for sprinkling

Set a large skillet over low heat. Add the oil, and then add the chile, ginger, and garlic and sauté for 5 minutes, until softened but not browned. Increase the heat to medium, add the chicken strips, and fry for a couple of minutes, turning with a spatula, until the chicken turns opaque.

Add the stock and the beans, and gently simmer for 10 to 15 minutes, until the beans are tender but not soggy. Add the coconut milk and stir well until heated through.

Serve sprinkled with the cilantro.

Creamy Spinach- and-Mushroom Lasagna

A great dish for entertaining, the lasagna will take about 50 minutes to prepare, but can be assembled well in advance and simply popped in the oven prior to eating. How simple is that? If you can get hold of it, use Italian "00" flour, a very soft, finely ground and sieved flour. Allow a good hour extra for making the pasta dough as it needs time to rest and dry, or substitute ready-made fresh pasta noodles. Serve it with an obligingly easy bowl of salad leaves and some crusty bread.

Serves 4

PASTA

¾ cup (100 grams) all-purpose flour

Pinch of fine sea salt

1 large egg

BÉCHAMEL SAUCE

3 cups (700 milliliters) whole milk

3 bay leaves

2 sprigs fresh rosemary

3 black peppercorns

3 tablespoons unsalted butter

½ cup (40 grams) all-purpose flour

Fine sea salt

VEGETABLE FILLING

2 tablespoons olive oil

5 cups (230 grams) perpetual spinach beet with any tough stalks removed, finely chopped (substitute Swiss chard)

1 large garlic clove, chopped

2 tablespoons unsalted butter

6 ounces (150 grams) oyster mushrooms

1 tablespoon Marsala

Fine sea salt and freshly ground pepper

8 ounces (200 grams) cream cheese

½ cup (60 grams) freshly grated Parmesan cheese

For the pasta: Stir together the flour and salt in a large mixing bowl. Make a well in the center of the flour mixture and crack the egg into it. Start beating the egg into the flour with a fork. When nearly all the flour is incorporated, use your hands to form it into a ball of dough.

Flour a board and knead the dough vigorously until it is silky and smooth, for about 5 minutes. Pop the dough into a plastic bag and put it in the fridge to rest for half an hour.

Divide the dough into 8 equal-size pieces, and roll each piece out thinly to make a sheet roughly 7 x 5 inches. The thinness should allow you to see your hand through the sheet. Feel free to use a pasta machine for this. Lay the pasta on a clean tea towel and leave to dry for half an hour while you prepare the other ingredients.

(continued on next page)

For the béchamel sauce: Combine the milk and the bay leaves, rosemary, and peppercorns in a small, heavy saucepan over a low heat and slowly bring to a boil. Remove from the heat and set aside to allow the milk to infuse with the herbs. In another small saucepan set over medium heat, melt the butter. Add the flour, and cook for a couple of minutes, stirring continuously, until the roux turns a toasty brown and smells fragrant. When the milk has cooled slightly, remove the herbs and gradually add the milk to the flour roux, whisking between each addition, until the sauce is smooth and glossy. Season well with salt and set aside.

For the filling: Heat the oil in a large skillet over medium heat. Add the spinach beet and garlic and sauté until the spinach beet is tender, for about 5 minutes. Transfer the spinach to a sieve set over a bowl and squeeze out as much excess water as possible.

In the same skillet, melt the butter over medium heat. Add the mushrooms and Marsala and a generous sprinkling of salt and pepper. Sauté for 3 to 4 minutes, making sure the mushrooms retain a bit of "bite." Remove from heat and set aside.

Perpetual Spinach Beet

An absolutely no-effort vegetable, perpetual spinach beet is as reliable as its name suggests. Caterpillars ignore it, and apart from the occasional hen pecking, there are leaves for the picking all year round. Sown in spring, the first young leaves, ready in just a matter of weeks, are great tossed in salads. As the plants mature, the leaves can be treated in the same way as chard or true spinach: steamed or wilted in butter, or tucked into a creamy lasagna. Spinach beet is an old European strain of chard, highly prized by gardeners for its longevity but not often seen for sale. Regular chard can be used instead, if you just use the green leaf and reserve the thick stalks for another recipe.

Set a pot of salted water to boil, and cook the dried pasta sheets for about a minute, in batches if necessary, so there's no danger that they'll stick together like a clump of damp laundry. Using a slotted spoon, lift the pasta sheets out of the boiling water and drain on a clean tea towel.

To assemble: Preheat the oven to 400°F (200°C).

Have the pasta, spinach, mushrooms, cream cheese, béchamel, and Parmesan at hand. Sprinkle one-third of the mushrooms over the bottom of a rectangular baking dish, 9 x 11 inches or equivalent. Add one-third of the spinach in evenly spaced teaspoonfuls, and dot with half a dozen large teaspoonfuls cream cheese. Season with salt and pepper. Drizzle one-quarter of the béchamel over the top, sprinkle with one-quarter of the Parmesan, then cover with a layer of pasta. Repeat twice more then finish with a final layer of bèchamel to completely cover the top layer of pasta and sprinkle with Parmesan. There may well be a sheet or two of pasta left over, depending on the size of your dish.

Bake uncovered until the top is golden and bubbling, about 30 minutes.

Summer Fruit Puffs

A basketful of fresh strawberries, raspberries, and currants barely needs a recipe, just a sprinkling of sugar and a swirl of cream. For something a little more substantial, these sweet batter puffs cradle a puddle of tart berries, with room for a scoop of vanilla ice cream on top.

Serves 6

Shortening or butter for greasing (a high smoking point is important)

¾ cup (100 grams) all-purpose flour

Pinch fine sea salt

2 large eggs

½ cup (150 milliliters) whole milk

2 tablespoons castor (superfine) sugar

6 ounces (150 grams) summer fruits (any combination of strawberries, raspberries, and red or black currants), roughly chopped and sprinkled with a tablespoon of superfine sugar

Preheat the oven to 425°F (220°C).

Measure ½ teaspoon of shortening or oil in each compartment of a 6-cup muffin tray.

Sift together the flour and salt into a mixing bowl. Make a well in the center and crack the eggs into it. Using an electric mixer, gradually beat the eggs into the flour. As the mixture gets sticky, start to gradually add the milk. Beat until all the milk is incorporated and the batter is smooth. Stir in the sugar.

Put the muffin tray in the hot oven until the melted fat is just smoking but not burning, about 3 minutes. Remove it from the oven.

Working quickly, divide the batter among the muffin compartments, filling them not more than a third of the way full. Listen for a sizzle as the batter hits the hot fat. Quickly put a heaping spoon of fruit in the middle of each pool of batter and return the tray to the oven for 20 minutes. Resist opening the oven while they are baking; otherwise they may deflate. When they are done, they should be well-risen and golden.

Serve while warm. The middles will sink as they cool, but that's the perfect place for cream or ice cream!

Strawberry Meringues

If your fridge, like mine, is littered with anonymous containers and bowls of saved food that could come in handy someday, I can almost guarantee one of those cartons will be filled with egg whites. Meringue is the solution. The first time I tried this recipe I used chopped fresh strawberries. As their juices ran during the cooking, the meringues began to wobble and were left stranded in a syrupy puddle. It was unpresentable, but delicious. Undeterred, for my next attempt I dried the strawberries first. It's rather agonizing to watch the plump, juicy berries shrivel before your eyes, but I think the end result is worth it: heaps of crisp sugary meringue, sticky centers, and slivers of chewy strawberry. You can easily substitute store-bought dehydrated strawberries.

Makes 6

1 pound (450 grams) strawberries, hulled and dried
   (see note), or 2 ounces dehydrated strawberries

2 large egg whites, at room temperature

Pinch fine sea salt

½ cup (100 grams) castor (superfine) sugar

. . . .

Preheat the oven to 200°F (100°C). Line a baking sheet with parchment paper.

In a very clean, dry mixing bowl without any hint of grease to prevent the whites from rising, combine the egg whites and salt, and beat with an electric mixer until they form stiff peaks, about 2 minutes. Add half of the sugar and beat again for about 1 minute until the peaks are stiff and glossy. Fold in the remaining sugar with a spatula. Fold in the dried strawberries.

Divide the meringue mixture into 6 large heaps on the prepared baking sheet, and bake for about 3 hours. When done, the meringues should be crisp on the outside and slightly chewy in the middle.

Note: To dry strawberries, preheat the oven to 200°F (100°C). Slice the strawberries thinly, between ¼- and ⅛-inch thick. Lay the slices flat on an oven-proof wire cooling rack set over a rimmed baking sheet. Place the baking sheet in the oven and let the strawberry slices slowly dry for about 2 hours, until they have a pliable, leathery texture. Remove strawberries from oven and maintain oven temperature for baking the meringues.

Strawberry Sorbet

Strawberries spoil very quickly once picked, so this easy, refreshing sorbet, which doesn't require an ice cream maker, is perfect for keeping up with the harvest. The addition of whipped egg white (see note below) gives it a soft, light texture, which scoops easily straight from the freezer. The sorbet will keep in the freezer for about a week.

Makes 1 pint (480 milliliters)

Juice of 2 limes (rolling or lightly pounding the limes on the counter with your palms will help to extract maximum juice)

¾ cup (150 grams) granulated sugar

1 pound (450 grams) strawberries, hulled and coarsely chopped

1 large egg white

Combine the lime juice and sugar in a small saucepan set over medium heat. Bring to a boil, stirring until the sugar has dissolved, then let the syrup boil undisturbed for 2 minutes. Pour into a mixing bowl to cool.

Put the strawberries in a blender or food processor and purée until smooth. Set a fine mesh sieve over the mixing bowl of syrup and let the strawberries strain into the bowl to extract the seeds. Stir well to combine, then pour into an open shallow plastic or glass container and freeze for about 2 hours, until it has a slushy half-frozen consistency.

In a very clean, dry mixing bowl, without any hint of grease to prevent the whites from rising, whip the egg white with an electric mixer for about 1 minute until soft peaks form.

Remove the sorbet from the freezer. Whisk the sorbet with a fork to break up the ice crystals. Spoon out the whipped egg white onto the partially frozen sorbet and, using a spatula, fold in the egg white until fully incorporated.

Return the sorbet to the freezer, then after about an hour, whisk for a final time when the sorbet has reached the slushy stage again. Cover and leave for at least 2 hours to freeze, before serving.

If using an ice cream maker, cool the strawberry syrup mixture completely, then add the whipped egg white. Process according to the manufacturer's directions.

Note: When juicing citrus, rolling or lightly pounding the fruits on the counter with your palms will help to extract maximum juice. Slightly warm or room-temperature fruits are easier to juice.

Due to the slight risk of salmonella, raw eggs should not be consumed by the very young, very old, infirm, or expectant mothers.

Strawberry Shortcake

The addition of strawberries turns a classic Christmas shortcake into a summery treat, perfect for afternoon tea. When you dry strawberries it really intensifies their flavor, and there's nothing nicer than finding sweet little nuggets in a mouthful of buttery shortcake. Follow the instructions for drying on page 115, or substitute purchased dried strawberries.

Serves 8 to 10

2¼ cups (280 grams) self-rising flour

½ cup (60 grams) cornstarch

½ cup (110 grams) castor (superfine) sugar

1 cup (225 grams) unsalted butter, at room temperature

1 pound (450 grams) fresh strawberries, dried (page 115)

or 2 ounces (50 grams) dried strawberries

Preheat the oven to 300°F (160°C).

Grease and line an 8-inch round cake pan, preferably a springform pan with a removable bottom.

Combine all the dry ingredients in a mixing bowl and stir to mix well. Add the butter. Using an electric mixer on slow speed, beat in the butter until the mixture resembles coarse breadcrumbs.

Coarsely chop the dried strawberries.

Pour half of the flour mixture into the prepared pan (the surface should be lumpy) and scatter the strawberries over. Pour the remaining flour mixture over the strawberries and press down firmly with the back of a spoon to smooth the entire surface. Score 10 equal slices with the tip of a sharp knife.

Bake for 25 to 30 minutes, or until pale golden at the edges. Leave in the pan to cool completely before releasing the sides and lifting out the cake.

Basic Ice Cream

This is a basic recipe to which you can add all sorts of puréed summer fruits. I improvise with whichever fruit is ripe in the garden and needs using. Vanilla sugar can be found in gourmet food and specialty kitchen stores. However, to make true, unadulterated vanilla ice cream, omit the vanilla sugar and instead take the trouble to infuse the milk with half a vanilla pod, scraping the tiny seeds into the custard mix before discarding the pod.

Makes 1 pint vanilla (475 milliliters) or 1 quart fruit ice cream (950 milliliters)

1 cup (300 milliliters) whole milk

1 vanilla pod, split in half lengthwise (optional; see headnote)

4 large egg yolks, whites reserved for another use

¼ cup (50 grams) castor (superfine) sugar

2 teaspoons vanilla sugar

1½ cups (14 ounces or 400 grams) puréed fruit (if using)

Heat the milk (and vanilla pod if using) in a saucepan, to hot but not boiling, then remove from the heat. Beat the egg yolks with the sugars until pale and creamy. Gradually add a couple of tablespoons of the warm milk, stirring vigorously with a wooden spoon to keep the eggs from curdling while the warm milk tempers the eggs. Pour the warmed beaten eggs into the saucepan with the milk, and stirring constantly, cook on the very lowest setting until the custard thickens enough to coat the back of the spoon. (This process is akin to watching paint dry, but do not get impatient and turn the heat up. If the mixture is allowed to boil, the eggs will begin to separate and scramble.) Remove from the heat.

Let your perfectly smooth custard cool to room temperature, then stir in the fruit purée (if using) and refrigerate the custard until it is completely cold. Transfer the custard to an ice cream maker and freeze according to manufacturer's instructions.

Plum and Marzipan Ice Cream

Ripe plums are delicious eaten straight from the tree, skin and flesh still warm from the sun, quintessentially sweet and syrupy. But all too quickly they pass their fleeting best to become a feast for wasps. This ice cream captures their essence in the freezer. It combines a basic vanilla custard with baked spiced plums and chunks of marzipan, for those who love to uncover chewy bits in their ice cream.

Serves 6 to 8

1 ¼ pounds (500 grams) purple or red plums

¼ cup (50 grams) light brown muscovado sugar (unrefined sugar with a molasses flavor)

2 teaspoons pumpkin pie spice, or a similar blend of nutmeg, ginger and cinnamon

1 recipe Basic Ice Cream custard, chilled (page 119)

4 ounces (100 grams) marzipan, crumbled into small chunks

Preheat the oven to 350°F (180°C).

Wash and halve the plums, and remove the stones. Put the plum halves in a covered baking dish, sprinkle with the sugar and the spices, and bake, covered, until soft, about 30 minutes. Transfer the cooked plums to a blender or food processor and purée until smooth. (You should have about 2 cups of puréed fruit.) Set aside to cool.

Combine the chilled Basic Ice Cream custard with the plum purée and chill for 30 minutes until cold.

Transfer the custard to an ice cream maker and freeze according to manufacturer's instructions. Alternatively, pour the custard into a freezer-safe flat dish and chill for a couple of hours in the freezer, until ice crystals begin to form. Remove the dish from the freezer and break up the custard with a balloon whisk, beating until smooth. Return to the freezer and repeat 2 or 3 times over a couple of hours until the ice cream reaches the desired consistency.

Stir in the marzipan chunks and serve, or cover and freeze the ice cream for up to 3 months.

Plum and Rhubarb Curd Tart

When plums are in season, make sure you always have a box of puff pastry in the freezer to make this family dessert: juicy baked plums on a pastry shell. Don't let an unavailability of rhubarb curd put you off; just use readily-available lemon curd instead. As summer progresses, keep your eyes open for blackberries growing wild, and make the same tart with lemon curd and a layer of blackberries, sprinkled with nutmeg and sugar. Serve the tart warm, with cream or vanilla custard.

Serves 4

6 ounces (150 grams) ready made-puff pastry, all butter if possible, thawed in the refrigerator

8 ounces (200 grams) Rhubarb Curd (page 60) or substitute purchased lemon curd

8 purple or red plums (about 1 pound or 450 grams), halved, each half cut into 10 slices

1 tablespoon castor (superfine) sugar

½ teaspoon ground ginger

Preheat oven to 400°F (200°C). Line a baking sheet with parchment paper.

On a floured work surface, roll out the pastry into a 6 x 9-inch rectangle between ¼- and ⅛-inch thick. Transfer the pastry to the baking sheet. Score a border, without cutting all the way through, ½-inch from the edge all the way around the rectangle.

Spread the rhubarb curd over the base within the scored border. Arrange the plum slices on their sides, slightly overlapping, in straight rows the length of the tart.

Mix together the sugar and ginger, and sprinkle evenly over the plums.

Bake for 25 to 30 minutes, until the plums are tender. Serve warm.

Real Fruit Gelatin Salad

Popular with children and adults alike, chilled fruit jellies made with real fruit are miles away from anything sticky that comes out of a box. Have fun setting them in individual dishes with fruit in the bottom, or in egg cups for a dolls' tea party.

Serves 4

1 pound (450 grams) mixed summer fruits (strawberries, red currants, raspberries, blackcurrants)

½ cup (100 grams) castor (superfine) sugar

¾ cup (200 milliliters) apple juice

Gelatin sheets, as needed

. . . .

Combine the fruit with the sugar in a large saucepan. Add ¾ cup (200 milliliters) water and bring to a rolling boil over medium-low heat. Reduce heat and simmer gently for 5 minutes, until the fruit is just soft. Pour through a sieve set over a bowl and collect as much juice as possible, reserving the fruit in the sieve. Add the apple juice to the bowl.

Measure the juice in the bowl: for every ½ cup (100 milliliters), use 1 gelatin sheet.

Soak the gelatin sheets in cold water to cover for 5 minutes, or until softened. Squeeze out the excess water and gradually add the sheets to the hot fruit juice, stirring as they dissolve.

Pour fruit juice into a jelly mold or ramekins, add the cooked fruit if desired, and refrigerate for at least 4 hours to set.

Tomato Sauce

This is a great basic tomato sauce. Simmering the tomatoes concentrates their sun-ripened flavor. Spread it thinly on pizzas or use as a pasta sauce, spiced up with extra anchovies or chiles. Put some away in the freezer too; it makes the perfect base for a classic Minestrone (page 156).

Makes 1 pint

2¼ pounds (1 kilogram) large ripe tomatoes (about 7 or 8; beefsteak tomatoes work well), or 2 (15½-ounce) cans good-quality tomatoes

3 tablespoons extra-virgin olive oil

5 garlic cloves, thinly sliced

2 teaspoons granulated sugar

4 anchovy fillets

Fine sea salt and freshly ground pepper

Quarter the tomatoes and cut out and discard any hard green cores. Coarsely chop the tomatoes and set aside in a bowl.

Combine the oil and sliced garlic in a large, heavy skillet over medium heat and sauté for about 5 minutes, stirring occasionally, until the garlic is soft but not browned. (Garlic should always be warmed with the oil to keep it from browning and burning too quickly.)

Add the chopped tomatoes, sugar, and anchovies to the skillet and stir well to incorporate. Reduce the heat to low and simmer uncovered for about 40 minutes, stirring regularly with a spatula, crushing the tomatoes as you do so. If the tomatoes begin to spit or stick to the skillet, turn the heat down further.

When the tomatoes have reduced to a very thick sauce (times may vary according to how juicy your tomatoes are), season with salt and pepper, and use as desired.

Herbed Focaccia

There are very few lunchtimes in the summer when I am not entirely satisfied with a handful of mixed salad greens from the garden, drenched with a good dressing, and fresh homemade bread to mop up the juices. If I am dissatisfied, it usually has more to do with the weather than the food. This focaccia is studded with black olives and rosemary, but works equally well with feta cheese and cherry tomatoes or anchovy and marjoram, and serves as comfort food on rainy or otherwise gloomy days. It's best devoured while still warm, but if there are any leftovers, pop them in the freezer and reheat in the oven to serve.

Makes 1 large loaf

1 recipe Basic Bread dough, salt omitted and allowed
    to double in bulk (page 54)

1 large egg

¾ cup (100 grams) pitted black olives (I use Italian ones
    marinated in garlic, but any would be suitable)

12 small sprigs fresh rosemary

2 tablespoons olive oil

Coarse sea salt

Preheat oven to 475°F (240°C). Grease a 12 x 8-inch (or close equivalent) baking sheet.

Turn the risen dough out onto a well-floured board, make a well in the center, and crack the egg into the hollow. Bring the edges of the dough into the center, gradually kneading in the egg. This is meant to be a sticky job; egg will ooze everywhere. Don't be tempted to add more flour as this will make the bread denser; just persevere. Wash and flour your hands halfway through if necessary. Eventually, when the egg is fully incorporated, the dough should be very soft and smooth. Once you have a smooth, almost manageable bulk, shape it to cover

the base of the greased baking sheet. Cover with a damp cloth and leave in a warm place to rise a second time, for 30 to 40 minutes until doubled in bulk.

When it looks nicely puffed up, press the olives and rosemary into the dough, covering the surface evenly. Don't be too gentle in pressing in the topping; you want to create small hollows to collect puddles of the olive oil. Drizzle the oil over the top followed by a generous sprinkling of coarse sea salt crystals. Bake for about 15 minutes, or until the focaccia is golden-brown. Remove from the baking sheet as soon as it is cool enough to handle to keep the bottom crust from becoming soggy. Cool on a wire rack.

Fresh Tomato and Basil Bread

I made this when I wanted an interesting bread to accompany a simple green salad with creamy white goat cheese. Smoked paprika gives it a wonderful depth of flavor and color. The soft dough is flecked with bits of sun-ripened tomatoes and aromatic basil.

Makes 1 loaf

8 ounces (225 grams) cherry tomatoes

4 ½ cups (450 grams) unbleached bread flour

1 teaspoon fine sea salt

1 teaspoon smoked paprika

1 teaspoon freshly ground pepper

1 tablespoon granulated sugar

2 teaspoons active dry yeast

1 large egg

About 1 ¼ cups (300 milliliters) whole milk, at room temperature

Olive oil for greasing

A handful of torn fresh basil leaves

Quarter each tomato and squeeze the juice and seeds from each quarter into a sieve set over a large glass measuring cup. Discard the seeds. (Or, if you are wistfully marveling that each seed is a potential new plant, save them for next year's tomato crop!) Coarsely chop the tomatoes.

Combine the flour, salt, paprika, and pepper in a large mixing bowl; stir with a fork to mix. Make a well in the center of the flour mixture and add the sugar and yeast.

Crack the egg into the measuring cup containing the tomato juice, beat the egg lightly with a fork, and add enough milk to make 10 ounces or 1¼ cup (300 milliliters). Pour about a third of the milk mixture into the flour well, stirring with a fork to just incorporate the yeast. Leave for 5 minutes, until the yeast begins frothing. Add the remaining milk to the flour mixture and stir with a fork to combine, then use your hands to form a soft dough. Transfer the dough to a lightly floured board and knead for 2 to 3 minutes. Wipe out the mixing bowl, lightly oil it, and put the dough back in. Cover with a damp cloth and leave in a warm place to rise for about an hour, or until doubled in bulk.

Once the dough has doubled in bulk, transfer it to the floured board. Make a depression in the center of the dough and add the tomatoes and the basil. Knead the dough briefly until they are fully incorporated. Shape into a round loaf, place on a baking sheet dusted with flour, and leave in a warm place again, for about an hour, to double in size.

Preheat oven to 400°F (200°C). Bake the loaf for 25 minutes, until the top is crisp and it sounds hollow when tapped on the base. Transfer to a wire rack to cool.

Scallion Breadsticks

These are great for pre-lunch drinks, with a crisp shell and a hint of softness on the inside. Just make sure there's something to dip them into, like the Chile and Cream Cheese Dip (page 136), or Herbed Mousse (page 16). They're best served straight from the oven, but if you want to make them in advance, they freeze well and can be heated up before serving. Fresh chives make a good substitute for scallions.

Makes 20

½ recipe Pizza Dough (page 52), left to rise once

Polenta or coarse cornmeal for dusting

3 or 4 scallions, chopped (white and green parts)

After the dough has doubled in size, punch it down and transfer it to a floured board.

Dust a large baking sheet generously with polenta.

Flatten the dough with your hands, sprinkle over a tablespoonful of the scallions and knead them into the dough. Repeat until all the onions are incorporated.

Press or roll the dough into a rectangle about 8 x 10 inches and ½-inch thick. Cut into thin strips, about 20 in all. As you transfer each dough strip to the prepared baking sheet pull both ends slightly to lengthen it. Leave in a warm place on the baking sheet for 30 minutes to rise.

Preheat the oven to 400°F (200°C). Bake for 12 to 15 minutes, until the breadsticks are crisp and golden on the outside, but still a bit chewy on the inside. Keep warm to serve.

Chile Jam

The strength of character of this cheerful little preserve will depend entirely on the kind of chiles you grow. I live close to a chile farm that offers choices of over one hundred varieties in its nursery, so this year I am experimenting with varying degrees of heat. For this recipe, I prefer to use a medium-strength chile that imparts a warm glow rather than a furious kick. You could use red jalapeños for a very mild heat or wrinkly skinned canned chipotles for a bit more of a kick. The end result should resemble a thick sauce rather than a solidified jelly, and will bring a vibrant touch of scarlet to the table. I eat it with all sorts of foods: cheese, omelets, stir-fries, or to liven up soups and sauces. The quantities below are enough for 2 cups (450 grams) of jam, but can be easily doubled or tripled.

Makes two 8-ounce (225 gram) jars

1½ pounds (600 grams) red bell peppers

2 tablespoons olive oil

3 tablespoons cider vinegar

4 medium-hot chiles, seeded with white membranes
    removed and discarded, finely chopped

½ cup (100 grams) granulated sugar

Fine sea salt

....

Preheat oven to 425°F (220°C). Prepare 2 glass canning jars by washing and sterilizing them (see page 61 for instructions).

Quarter and core the red peppers and arrange them skin-side down on a baking sheet. Drizzle the olive oil over the peppers and roast in the oven for 10 minutes. Turn the peppers over and continue to roast until the skins start to blister and blacken, for about 10 minutes. Remove the baking sheet from the oven and pop the peppers while they are still hot into a resealable plastic bag for a few minutes to steam. The skins can then easily be peeled off. No need to be pedantic about this; a few remaining obstinate scraps of skin won't matter.

Place the peeled roasted peppers in a blender or food processor, add the vinegar, and purée to a smooth pulp.

Combine the roasted pepper purée, chopped chiles, and sugar in a medium, heavy saucepan over medium heat, stirring until all the sugar has dissolved. Raise the heat and boil hard for 5 minutes, stirring so that the pepper mixture doesn't stick to the bottom of the pan. Cool slightly and season to taste with salt. Carefully pour the jam into the warm sterilized jars.

Stored in the refrigerator, the jam will keep for 4 months. Use within 2 months after opening.

Chile and Cream Cheese Dip

Long, lazy summer days and drinks in the garden go hand in hand with a stream of quickly assembled dips and platefuls of chopped raw vegetables to dig into them. The bright red chile jam looks great swirled through the cream cheese. Serve with sticks of celery, carrot, and cucumber, or warm Scallion Breadsticks (page 132).

Serves 4

½ cup (125 grams) cream cheese, at room temperature

½ cup (125 grams) plain Greek-style yogurt

3 tablespoons Chile Jam (page 134), or substitute a sweet chile dipping sauce, available in the Asian food section of most supermarkets

Using a fork, mix together the cream cheese and yogurt until fully combined. Transfer to a serving bowl and gently swirl the chile jam through the mixture, creating a marbled effect.

Pink Grapefruit Dressing

Makes ½ cup (120 milliliters)

Juice of ½ pink grapefruit

¼ cup (60 milliliters) extra-virgin olive oil

1 teaspoon chopped fresh dill

1 tablespoon chopped fresh chives

Fine sea salt and freshly ground pepper

Combine all the ingredients in a clean glass jar, screw the lid on tightly, and give it a good shake to blend. Adjust seasonings to taste.

Roasted Garlic Vinaigrette

Makes ½ cup (120 milliliters)

1 large head garlic

6 tablespoons extra-virgin olive oil, divided

1 tablespoon balsamic vinegar

1 tablespoon freshly squeezed lemon juice

Fine sea salt and freshly ground pepper

Preheat oven to 400°F (200°C).

Slice about ¼-inch off the top of the garlic head, just far enough down to cut the tips off the individual cloves. Place the garlic on a square of foil large enough to encase the whole head and drizzle the cut surfaces with 2 teaspoons of the olive oil. Wrap the foil tightly around the garlic, place in a small baking dish, and bake for about 30 minutes, until the garlic feels soft when squeezed. Unwrap and let sit until cool enough to handle.

Squeeze the softened garlic pulp into a blender or food processor, discarding the skins. Add the remaining 4 tablespoons olive oil, balsamic vinegar, and lemon juice and blend until smooth. Season to taste with salt and pepper. Will keep for a week stored in the fridge in a sealed container.

Garlic

No garden need be without garlic: four cloves will grow in a twelve-inch pot on a balcony. Having in the past planted whatever was malingering in the corner of my vegetable bowl, this year I'm doing it properly. I'm growing Spanish Red and Rosso di Sulmona, an Italian garlic from Abruzzo. Both are hard-neck varieties which, in garlic-speak, means they will only keep for three or four months but should have fewer, larger cloves per head. They should be perfect for roasting, a method which minimizes their pungency and intensifies their sweetness. Roll on July!

Elderflower Cordial

By May, I begin to equip the car with my essential tool kit of garden shears and carrier bags. As I am rambling along the local country lanes, I make a mental note of all the promising elderflower bushes, and wait until their lacy flower heads are just perfectly mid-bloom: they'll be creamy in color and can be shaken without dropping any petals. Don't be put off by any unpleasant musky aroma; as they steep with the sugar and lemon, they will transform, Cinderella-style, into the most delicate taste of summer. Diluted with water, elderflower cordial is a traditional British and Northern European refresher, popular since Victorian times. The sweet syrup can be drizzled over ice cream, summer berries, or warm pancakes. The high sugar content prevents the syrup from freezing, so it can be coaxed out of the bottle straight from the freezer, making it perfect for unexpected guests.

Makes 5 1/4 pints (2.5 liters)

13 cups (2.5 kilograms) granulated sugar

35 elderflower heads, each cluster with a short stalk for handling

3 1/2 ounces (100 grams) citric acid (see note, page 141)

2 unwaxed lemons, sliced

Heat 8 1/2 cups (2 liters) of water and the sugar in a large saucepan or pot, stirring until the sugar has completely dissolved. Set aside to cool.

While the syrup is cooling, shake the elderflower heads to evict anything that boasts legs.

Stir the citric acid into the cooled syrup, then add the lemon slices and flower heads. Cover the saucepan with a cloth and leave to steep for 2 to 3 days. Stir the mixture gently two or three times a day.

Prepare enough glass bottles with tightly fitting lids to hold the cordial (see page 61 for instructions on sterilizing). Strain the liquid through a clean muslin, cheesecloth, or tea towel and pour into the sterilized bottles. The cordial should have a syrupy consistency and will keep for a few months in a cool dark place. Alternatively, it freezes well. To freeze, fill plastic bottles, leaving room for expansion.

To serve, dilute with ice-cold sparkling water, and add ice and a slice of lemon to the glass.

Note: Citric acid, sometimes referred to as sour salt, is a white powder derived from pineapples, citrus, and other acidic fruits. You can generally find it in pharmacies or order it online.

Elderflower Fizz

To add a bit of a kick to your elderflower cordial, pour this for your guests on a summer's evening. The recipe can obviously be adjusted for small or large crowds.

1 part elderflower cordial

1 part white rum

6 parts sparkling lemonade

Lots of ice

A few mint leaves, for serving

A slice of lemon for each glass

· ·

Put the elderflower cordial and rum in a tall glass, add a few cubes of ice, then top up with the lemonade to taste. Serve with a slice of lemon, a couple of mint leaves, and a warm evening.

Enjoy!

Strawberry and Elderflower Jam

I like my strawberry jam bursting with fruitiness, rich red in color, and only just firm enough to balance on top of a scone. This recipe for a tart jam with a hint of elderflower is a perfect summer's day in a jar. It has a very low sugar content, so it should be kept in the fridge. There's absolutely no danger of it hanging around too long in our house though; it's the favorite topping for croissants, scones, and pancakes, morning, noon, and night.

Makes two 12-ounce (340 gram) jars

2 ¼ pounds (1 kilogram) strawberries, hulled and coarsely chopped

1 ¼ cups (300 milliliters) elderflower cordial (page 140), or substitute

    1 ½ cups (275 grams) castor (superfine) sugar and 1 tablespoon rosewater

Prepare two 12-ounce glass canning jars by washing and sterilizing them. (See page 61 for instructions.)

Put strawberries in a heavy, wide-bottomed pot. Add the elderflower cordial or sugar and rosewater and stir until completely combined.

Bring to a boil over medium heat, then reduce heat and simmer for 15 to 20 minutes, stirring often to make sure the strawberries are not sticking to the bottom. Reduce the heat if necessary. You don't need to check for proper setting, as this jam doesn't really set. The consistency should be more like a thick sauce.

Spoon the jam into the warm sterilized glass jars. Screw on the metal lids while the jam is still hot, and allow to cool on the counter. The jam will keep, unopened, in the refrigerator, for 1 month, once opened it should be consumed within a week.

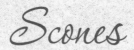

Scones

Now that you have the jam, you need the scones. Quick and easy to prepare, these have to be eaten while fresh and warm. Get the tea brewing!

Makes 1 dozen

2 ¼ cups (225 grams) all-purpose flour

Pinch of salt

4 teaspoons baking powder

¼ cup (55 grams) butter, at room temperature

2 tablespoons castor (superfine) sugar

1 large egg, at room temperature

6 tablespoons (75 milliliters) whole milk, at room temperature

Preheat the oven to 450°F (230°C). Line a baking sheet with parchment paper.

Combine the flour, salt, and baking powder in a mixing bowl and stir with a fork to blend. Cut or rub in the butter as gently as you can until it resembles coarse breadcrumbs. The less handling, the better. Stir in the sugar, and make a well in the center.

In a small bowl, beat the egg with a fork, then add the milk and whisk to blend. Pour about three-quarters of the liquid into the well in the mixing bowl. Mix the ingredients with a fork to form a dough. Add more liquid if necessary to make it just hold together. Reserve any leftover egg.

Transfer the dough to a floured board and lightly roll to about 1-inch thick. Cut into circles with a floured 2 ½-inch cookie cutter.

Place the dough circles on the prepared baking sheet, brush the tops with the leftover beaten egg, and bake for 8 to 10 minutes, until well-risen and golden.

Set the scones on a wire cooling rack and cover with a clean tea towel to keep them moist while they cool.

Scones are no good kept for more than a day, but leftovers keep well in the freezer.

Rhubarb and Ginger Jam

I have inherited a very prolific rhubarb patch so am always looking for ways to preserve the red stalks to last through the year. Rhubarb and ginger are a classic combination. The jam has a spicy warmth, and is great on toast, in trifles, or stirred into Greek yogurt.

Makes four 12-ounce (340-gram) jars

2 ¼ pounds (1 kilogram) rhubarb, preferably young
    red stalks

2 ¼ pounds (1 kilogram) granulated sugar

Juice of 2 lemons

2-inch piece fresh ginger, unpeeled

4 ounces (113 grams) preserved ginger, finely chopped (optional)

Trim and chop the rhubarb into 1-inch pieces. Combine the rhubarb, sugar, and lemon juice in a large bowl and mix well.

Bruise the piece of ginger by giving it a few thwacks with a rolling pin. Tie it in a small muslin bag, or in a square of cheesecloth. Nestle the ginger down in the rhubarb. Cover and refrigerate for at least 24 hours and up to 48 hours.

Prepare four 12-ounce glass canning jars by washing and sterilizing them. (See page 61 for instructions.)

Transfer the rhubarb mixture with the ginger to a large saucepan set over medium-high heat and bring to a boil. Boil rapidly for about 15 minutes, stirring frequently with a wooden spoon and checking to be sure the fruit doesn't burn on the bottom. If necessary, reduce the heat.

When the fruit is soft and transparent, test it for setting by spooning a small blob of jam onto a cold saucer. Place the saucer in the freezer for 1 to 2 minutes, then remove it and try touching the jam with your finger. If the surface wrinkles it's ready. If it hasn't begun to form a skin, continue to cook for another 2 to 3 minutes, and test again.

Remove the jam from the heat immediately, remove the piece of ginger, and stir in the chopped preserved ginger, if using. Spoon the jam into the warm sterilized glass jars. Screw on the metal lids while the jam is still hot, and allow to cool on the counter. The jam will keep, unopened, in a cool dry place for 12 months or opened, in the refrigerator, for 2 months.

Autumn

"Through cunning with dibble, rake, mattock and spade,

by line and by level trim garden is made."

— Thomas Tusser, 1524-1580

Gales forecasted and gales delivered.

Little bits of tree are scattered all over the garden. A white duck lost its footing on the chimney and landed *thud* in the study. Touchingly, on its first quack of freedom, its partner swooped down to join the sooty bird on the pond for a morning of preening.

The willow warblers with their olive green plumage are hovering over the fading annuals, feasting on insects before their long flight back to Africa.

The squash are soaking up the last of the sunshine, but need to be harvested before the first frosts. Of course there are also a few zucchini that have ended up giant-sized. My daughter's solution is to dress one up in a bonnet and shawl and push it around the garden in a baby buggy!

It feels good to get the garden tidied up for the winter: wilted annuals uprooted, seeds collected, and bean poles dismantled. The perennials I leave until the spring, to encourage self-seeding. Giant sunflower heads sway at the back of the border, a feast for the birds. The onions and shallots are now safely stored, and the ground is ready for planting broad beans and garlic.

Autumn

Side Dishes and Starters

Warm Pear-and-Walnut Salad

Minestrone

Very Vegetable Soup

Celery Root and Apple soup

Hazelnut Cream Cheese

Stir-Fried Sesame Leeks

Roasted Cauliflower

Potatoes Dauphinoise with Lemon Zest

Borlotti Beans on Toast

Mains

Chicken with Fennel and Leeks

Sausage and Leek Cannelloni

Basil–Walnut Pesto

Acorn Squash and Chorizo Risotto

Pork with Spiced Plums

Aromatic Basil Rice

Chicken with Apple-Cardamom Stuffing

Desserts

Apple Cake

Pear and Almond Cake

Butternut Squash and Pumpkin Seed Loaf

Hot Cross Kebabs

Currant Tea Loaf

Blackberry and Almond Scrunchies

Blackberry and Apple Ice Cream

Baked Orchard Fruits

Sundries

Savory Fennel-Seed Oat Biscuits

Poppy Seed Crackers

Best Walnut Biscuits

Pear and walnut focaccia

Crabapple and Herb Jelly

Raspberry Vinegar

Onion Marmalade

Blackberry Jelly

Quince Paste

Warm Pear-and-Walnut Salad

If you're beginning to tire of chomping your way through yet another row of salad leaves, and with the change of season yearn for something just a little more comforting, a warm salad is a good halfway house. Pears and walnuts are an earthy combination, and the feta adds a burst of saltiness. Serve with hunks of homemade bread.

Serves 4

1 tablespoon sunflower oil

1 cup (100 grams) walnut halves

1 tablespoon balsamic vinegar

1 teaspoon freshly ground pepper

2 firm pears, peeled, cored, and cut into ¾-inch chunks

1 tablespoon honey

8 ounces (200 grams) feta cheese, cubed

Fine sea salt

4 large handfuls mixed salad leaves (lettuce, spinach, arugula, mâche), for serving

Honey–Mustard Vinaigrette (page 59) for drizzling, or other dressing of your choice (optional)

Heat the oil in a large skillet over medium heat. Add the walnuts, vinegar, and pepper and cook for 1 minute, shuffling the nuts around with a spatula. Add the pear chunks and the honey, and continue to stir for another few minutes, until the walnuts are lightly toasted and the pear is softened at the edges. Remove the skillet from the heat, add the feta cheese, stir to combine, and leave to cool slightly. Taste and season with salt, if necessary.

Sprinkle a handful of salad leaves on each plate, drizzle with vinaigrette, if using, then top with a heap of the warm pear-walnut mixture.

Minestrone

There is no definitive Italian recipe for minestrone. It's essentially a mixture of vegetables, dried beans, and any leftovers that need using. That makes it a perfect food for the gardener. A big pot continually topped off with more vegetables can supply lunch for six months of the year. This recipe has autumnal origins, making the most of celery, fennel, leeks, and fresh borlotti beans. Serve the soup with slabs of crusty homemade bread.

Serves 6

2 tablespoons olive oil

1 large garlic clove, finely sliced

1 large onion, diced

2 ribs celery, finely diced (about ½ cup or 75 grams)

½ bulb fennel (about 4 ounces or 100 grams), diced

2 carrots (about 10 ounces or 250 grams), quartere lengthwise and cut into ¼-inch slices

1 small parsnip (about 5 ounces or 150 grams), diced

1 leek (about 4 ounces or 100 grams), halved lengthwise and cut into ¼-inch slices

6 cups (1.5 liters) vegetable stock, heated and kept warm, divided

2 large beefsteak tomatoes (about 14 ounces or 400 grams), chopped; or substitute 1 (15½-ounce or 400-gram) can diced tomatoes

1 pound (450 grams) fresh borlotti beans; substitute 1 (15½-ounce or 400-gram) can borlotti or pinto beans, drained and rinsed

¼ head savoy cabbage (about 8 ounces or 250 grams), thinly sliced

2 ounces (50 grams) dried mini pasta shapes, or a mixture of different types

2 tablespoons chopped fresh marjoram or 1 teaspoon dried

2 tablespoons chopped fresh flat-leaf parsley (substitute 1 teaspoon dried basil)

Sea salt and freshly ground pepper

Freshly grated Parmesan cheese, for serving

Combine the olive oil and garlic in a large, heavy pot over medium-low heat. Add the onion, celery, and fennel and sauté for 5 minutes, stirring frequently with a spatula. Add the carrots, parsnip, and leek and continue to sauté gently for a further 10 minutes, until the vegetables are beginning to soften. If they are starting to brown, reduce the heat.

Add 4 cups (1.2 liters) of the stock, the chopped tomatoes, and the beans. Bring the soup to a boil, then reduce the heat to low and simmer, partially covered, for 45 minutes, stirring occasionally.

Add the cabbage and the pasta, and up to 2 cups (.5 liter) more stock, as necessary. Simmer for another 15 minutes until the cabbage and pasta are cooked. Taste and adjust the seasoning with salt and pepper.

Serve with freshly grated Parmesan cheese.

"He must have a poor eye for beauty who has not observed how much of it there is in the form and colour which cabbages and other plants of that genus exhibit through the various stages of growth and decay."

—William Wordsworth

Very Vegetable Soup

Take a wander around the garden in mid-autumn, collecting whatever is ripe, and you'd probably come up with this soup. The addition of an apple tempers the saltiness of the bacon. Serve with chunks of buttered warm brown bread.

Serves 4

2 tablespoons olive oil

1 large onion, chopped

4 garlic cloves, finely sliced

2 thick slices bacon (about 4 ounces or 100 grams), finely chopped

2 waxy potatoes, such as round white or red (about 12 ounces or 300 grams), cut into ½-inch cubes

Kernels from 1 cob sweet corn, sliced off, or 5 ounces (120 grams) frozen corn kernels

8 ounces (200 grams) rutabaga (swede), chopped into ½-inch cubes

1 apple (about 6 ounces or 150 grams, chopped

2 cups (600 milliliters) vegetable stock

4 fresh sage leaves, finely chopped, or ½ teaspoon dried

4 cavolo nero leaves or 2 kale or savoy cabbage leaves, ribs removed, sliced into ribbons

Sea salt and freshly ground pepper

Warm the oil in a large, heavy pot over low heat. Add the onion and garlic and cook for 5 minutes, until soft but not browned. Add the bacon and cook for a minute before adding the potatoes, sweet corn kernels, rutabaga and apple. Stir well, then add the stock and the sage. Cover and simmer very gently for 30 minutes, or until the vegetables are soft; the rutabaga will take the longest to cook. Add the cavolo nero and simmer, covered, for a further 5 minutes, until the cavolo nero is cooked but not soggy.

Taste for seasoning; the bacon may provide enough salt, but do add a twist of black pepper before serving.

Cavolo Nero

For the past couple of years I have been growing cavolo nero, a delicious kale from Tuscany. Not only does it give the garden an air of the fairy tale with its fountain of crinkled leaves, it also provides a cut-and-come-again crop for months on end, and, like all kale, it isn't bothered by cabbage white caterpillars.

Celery Root and Apple Soup

This resembles a hot version of a Waldorf salad in terms of flavor, but it is smooth and thick in consistency, and garnished with a little nutty knob of cream cheese blended with chopped toasted hazelnuts.

Serves 4 to 5

1 celery root (about 1¼ pounds or 550 grams)

Juice of ½ lemon

2 tablespoons unsalted butter

2 medium white onions, chopped

4 tablespoons (25 grams) all-purpose flour

1 dessert apple, such as Jonagold or Cox,
   peeled, cored, and grated

3½ cups (1 liter) vegetable stock

½ cup (100 milliliters) heavy whipping cream

Sea salt and freshly ground pepper

½ teaspoon freshly grated nutmeg

2 tablespoons chopped fresh flat-leaf parsley

1 recipe Hazelnut Cream Cheese (page 162)

Peel the celery root and cut into ½-inch pieces (you should have about 4 cups chopped). Immediately place the celery root pieces in a bowl and add water to cover. Add the lemon juice to prevent browning and let sit.

Melt the butter in a large, heavy pot over medium heat. Add the onions and sauté for 5 minutes, until softened but not browned.

Drain the celery root and transfer to a clean kitchen towel to dry. In a large bowl, toss the celery root with the flour to coat, then add it to the onions in the pot and cook for 5 minutes, stirring regularly with a spatula.

Add the apple and about three-quarters of the stock to the pot and bring to a boil. Reduce the heat to low and simmer gently for 30 minutes, until the celery root is really soft.

Transfer the soup to a blender or food processor and carefully process until completely smooth; return to the cooking pot. Alternatively, blend the soup in the pot using an immersion blender until completely smooth. Add the cream and some of the remaining stock, if necessary, to reach the desired consistency. Season with salt and pepper to taste, stir in the nutmeg and heat through but do not boil.

Top each serving with a sprinkling of chopped parsley and a dollop of Hazelnut Cream Cheese.

Celery Root

Celery root must be the ugliest of all vegetables. If you have only ever purchased the shrink-wrapped version in the grocery store, you would be amazed at how a wash and a shave will transform such a brute.

Celery root seeds are miniscule, and the first pair of tiny leaves look very tentative, but by mid-summer they will have produced a great bush of leaves above ground and a knobby root below the soil. It is similar in flavor to celery or fennel but with completely the opposite texture—soft and creamy— when cooked, which makes it ideal for thick soups.

Hazelnut Cream Cheese

I love this combination: smooth cheese blended with toasted hazelnuts. It works well as a dip with salads, spread on crusty bread, or as an alternative to croutons in a soup.

Serves 2 for dipping and spreading

1 teaspoon sunflower oil

3 tablespoons raw hazelnuts, skins removed if desired

Fine sea salt

4 ounces (150 grams) cream cheese, at room temperature

1 tablespoon plain Greek-style yogurt, if needed

Coarsely chop the hazelnuts, leaving them fairly uneven. Heat the oil in a small skillet over medium-low heat. Add the hazelnuts and a good pinch of salt, and toast for 2 minutes, stirring continuously. As soon as the nuts begin to brown, remove them from the heat and transfer them to a bowl.

Simply mix the nuts into the cheese. Cream cheese can vary quite a bit in texture, and depending on whether you want to spread, dip, or dollop it, add a spoonful of Greek yogurt to soften the consistency.

Stir-Fried Sesame Leeks

Leeks are great in a number of traditional preparations, but this low-on-fuss, high-on-aroma side dish has an Asian twist. It's delicious served with risotto, or plain boiled rice and stir-fried chicken. Make sure to always wash leeks thoroughly—there's nothing worse than a gritty mouthful. For this recipe, the best way is to slit them lengthwise starting from one inch above the base, then hold them upside down under a running tap and fan out the leaves to allow all the sand to rinse away. Shake dry and cut off the base.

Serves 4

1 pound (400 grams) leeks, green tops trimmed

2 tablespoons toasted sesame oil

1-inch piece fresh ginger, peeled and grated

1 teaspoon castor (superfine) sugar

1 tablespoon toasted sesame seeds

Fine sea salt and freshly ground pepper

Thinly slice the leeks lengthwise into strips about 6 to 8 inches long. If the leeks are very long, you may need to cut them in half (crosswise) as well.

Heat the sesame oil in a wok, or a large skillet over medium heat. Add the grated ginger and leeks and stir-fry for about 3 minutes, tossing the leeks frequently. Stirring leeks might seem akin to unraveling a bird's nest, but as the leeks soften they will become more manageable. When the leeks begin to soften and become translucent, add the sugar and sesame seeds along with a couple tablespoons of water. Continue to stir for another couple of minutes until most of the water has evaporated, then season to taste with salt and pepper. Serve immediately.

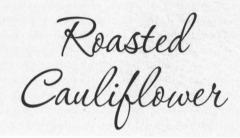

Roasted Cauliflower

Cauliflower is not one of my top ten vegetables; it's tricky to grow, and at a mere six inches tall it often falls prey to the chickens' destructive beaks. If I do have any heads left to harvest, I'll be roasting them by this simple method, which is much livelier than plain old boiled cauliflower.

Serves 4

½ head cauliflower, cut into florets

4 tablespoons olive oil

1 teaspoon chopped fresh thyme or ½ teaspoon dried

Sea salt and freshly ground pepper

A squeeze of lemon juice, for serving

Preheat the oven to 425°F (220°C).

Fill a pot with 1 inch of water. Place a steamer insert in the pot and bring the water to a boil. Alternatively, bring a large pot of water to boil. Add the cauliflower and boil or steam for 3 minutes, until tender-crisp.

Drain the cauliflower well and transfer to an ovenproof baking dish or rimmed baking sheet large enough to hold the florets in a single layer. Toss the florets with the olive oil and the thyme, and season well with the salt and pepper. Roast for 10 minutes, turning occasionally, until the florets are just turning brown and crispy around the edges, but are still firm in the center.

Squeeze the lemon juice over the cauliflower and serve.

Potatoes Dauphinoise with Lemon Zest

I love this dish derived from the classic French recipe: thin discs of potato are roasted in the oven with cream until they are crisp on the top and satisfyingly soft in the middle. In the summer, I make the same recipe using new potatoes instead, and add a handful of chopped mint.

Serves 4 to 6

2 pounds (1 kilogram) waxy potatoes, such as round white or red (about 6)

2 tablespoons olive oil, plus extra for drizzling

Grated zest of 1 lemon

Sea salt and freshly ground pepper

½ cup (150 milliliters) heavy whipping cream

½ cup (150 milliliters) hot water

Preheat the oven to 375°F (190°C).

Peel and cut the potatoes into ¼-inch-thick slices. Transfer the potatoes to a large mixing bowl and add the olive oil. Stir in the lemon zest and season with the salt and pepper.

Spread the potatoes in a wide, ovenproof dish, and shuffle them around a bit so the slices lie flat and look happily rustic rather than manicured.

Combine the cream and the hot water, and pour over the potatoes. Cover the dish with a sheet of aluminum foil and bake for 30 minutes. Remove the foil, drizzle with a little olive oil, and cook for a further 30 minutes, until the top is crisp and golden.

Borlotti Beans on Toast

An exhausting day spent gardening in the drizzle calls for a supper of comfort food, but one that doesn't come out of a can. These slow-cooked beans can be popped in the oven in the afternoon and will be beautifully soft and full of flavor by the time light stops its play. Dried pinto or cannellini beans would be a good substitute, soaked first according to the package instructions. Dried borlotti beans can be purchased from specialty stores, Italian markets, or are sold online from gourmet retailers.

Serves 4

2 pounds (1 kilogram) tomatoes

2 tablespoons olive oil, plus more for drizzling

2 cloves garlic, sliced

2 onions (about 8 ounces or 250 grams), chopped

1 pound (450 grams) shelled borlotti beans

    (about 2 pounds unshelled)

2 teaspoons smoked paprika

A few fresh sage leaves, torn into large pieces

1 cup (240 milliliters) dry white wine

Fine sea salt and freshly ground pepper

8 thick slices ciabatta bread, toasted

Preheat the oven to 300°F (150°C).

First, skin the tomatoes: Bring a large pot of water to a boil. Prepare an ice-water bath in a large bowl. Make a small slit in the skins of the tomatoes

(continued on next page)

167

with a knife, then drop them in the boiling water for 1 minute, just until the skins begin to split. Using a slotted spoon, transfer the tomatoes to the ice-water bath to stop the cooking. You should be able to pull the skins off easily with your fingers. Quarter the tomatoes and discard any hard cores.

Heat the oil in a large skillet over medium heat. Add the garlic and onions, and sauté for 5 minutes until the onions are soft and slightly transparent. Add the tomatoes and simmer for about 5 minutes, until they begin to soften.

Transfer the contents of the skillet to an oven-safe casserole with a lid. Add the beans, smoked paprika, sage, and wine. Season with salt and pepper. Add ½ cup (150 milliliters) of water and give everything a good stir to combine. Cover the casserole and bake for 2 hours. Check and stir the beans after 1 hour; add another ½ cup of water if they are becoming dry. After 2 hours, the beans should be beautifully tender. Taste and season, if necessary.

Serve on slices of toasted ciabatta and finish with a final drizzle of olive oil.

Borlotti Beans

I first grew borlotti beans because they are irresistible to paint, but hard to find in stores. Their mottled pods are perfect for watercolors. They look great in the garden too, climbing up rustic poles interlaced with sweet peas. But even better (something the Italians have known for generations), the creamy speckled beans inside the pods taste fantastic. They're best eaten fresh, but dry or freeze exceptionally well to extend their season. They can also be eaten as young green pods, but quite frankly there are plenty of other beans for that purpose, and you would be missing out on the beautiful magenta markings that appear on the pods as they mature.

Chicken with Fennel and Leeks

Crispy-skinned chicken with the spicy licorice flavor of fennel and the subtle sweetness of braised leeks is a true celebration of autumnal vegetables. I like the delicate tonal greens, so I keep with the theme and serve basmati rice and steamed spinach and cauliflower alongside. Feel free to increase the amount of chicken for heartier appetites, but do try to find pastured, naturally raised birds. They are a little more expensive, but they're also more healthful and delicious.

Serves 4

1 fennel bulb, halved lengthwise then sliced into eighths

2 small leeks (8 ounces or 250 grams), green tops trimmed and discarded, cut diagonally into 3-inch pieces

2 tablespoons olive oil

6 large chicken thighs, cut off the bone and halved

7 tablespoons (100 milliliters) white wine

7 tablespoons (100 milliliters) chicken or vegetable stock, heated and kept warm

Fine sea salt and freshly ground pepper

1 tablespoon each roughly chopped fresh dill and cilantro (coriander)

Preheat the oven to 400°F (200°C).

Set a pot with 1 inch of water to boil, and set a steamer insert inside.

Steam the fennel until tender, about 5 minutes. Transfer the fennel to a large roasting dish along with the leeks. You'll need enough room in the dish for the chicken and vegetables to lie in a single layer rather

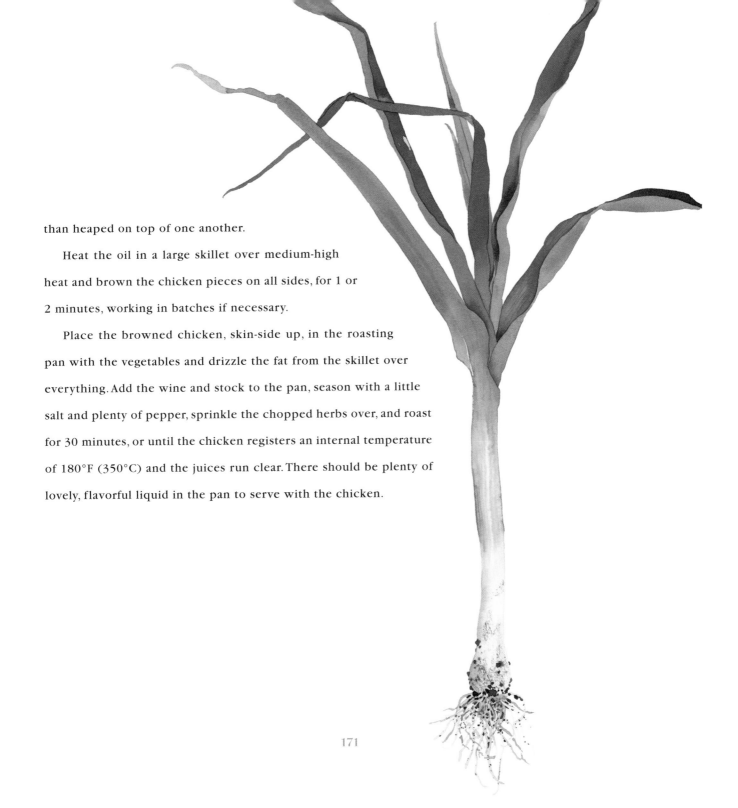

than heaped on top of one another.

Heat the oil in a large skillet over medium-high heat and brown the chicken pieces on all sides, for 1 or 2 minutes, working in batches if necessary.

Place the browned chicken, skin-side up, in the roasting pan with the vegetables and drizzle the fat from the skillet over everything. Add the wine and stock to the pan, season with a little salt and plenty of pepper, sprinkle the chopped herbs over, and roast for 30 minutes, or until the chicken registers an internal temperature of 180°F (350°C) and the juices run clear. There should be plenty of lovely, flavorful liquid in the pan to serve with the chicken.

Sausage and Leek Cannelloni

Cannelloni tubes make up the smallest percentage of the pasta sales market; it's likely that none of us can be bothered with the thought of stuffing them. This recipe is a great cheat: you simply roll up some pasta sheets around the stuffing. Bathed in a rich tomato sauce, this dish utilizes the classic British sausage–and–leek combination with Italian aspirations. Serve as a hearty supper with wilted spinach on the side.

Serves 4

PASTA DOUGH

(or substitute 8 dried lasagna noodles)

1 cup (100 grams) all-purpose flour

Pinch sea salt

1 large egg

FILLING

¼ cup (55 grams) butter

2 leeks (about 12 ounces or 300 grams trimmed weight),
white and green parts finely chopped

Sea salt and freshly ground pepper

1 pound (450 grams) best-quality pork sausages

1 recipe Tomato Sauce (page 127)

¼ cup (30 grams) freshly grated Parmesan cheese

Preheat the oven to 400°F (200°C).

For the pasta: Stir together the flour and salt in a large mixing bowl. Make a well in the center of the flour mixture and crack the egg into it. Start beating the egg into the flour with a fork. When nearly all the flour is incorporated, use your hands to form it into a ball of dough.

Flour a board and knead the dough vigorously until it is silky and smooth, for about 5 minutes. Pop the dough into a plastic bag and put it in the fridge to rest for half an hour.

Divide the dough into 8 equal-size pieces, and roll each piece out thinly to make a sheet roughly 7 x 5 inches. The thinness should allow you to see your hand through the sheet. Feel free to use a pasta machine for this. Lay the pasta on a clean tea towel and leave to dry for half an hour while you prepare the other ingredients.

Bring a large pot of salted water to boil and cook the pasta sheets for about a minute, in batches to keep them from sticking to one another. If using dried lasagna noodles, cook according to package directions until al dente. Using a slotted spoon, lift the pasta sheets out of the water and place them on a clean kitchen towel to drain.

For the filling: Melt the butter in a heavy skillet over medium heat and add the leeks, stirring to coat them in the butter. Press a layer of foil directly onto the leeks and reduce the heat to its lowest setting. Cook for about 30 minutes, checking occasionally, until the leeks are very soft. Season well with salt and pepper.

Slice into the casings of the sausages and pull them off. Divide the sausage meat into 8 portions. Take a sheet of pasta and spread the sausage meat in a line across the center, top with one-eighth of the leeks, then roll the sheet up to encase the filling in a tube. Trim off any excess, so the pasta just overlaps; you don't want a complete double layer of pasta. Repeat with the remaining lasagna noodles.

Place the filled tubes, seam-side down, in a single layer in an ovenproof dish, and pour the tomato sauce over the top. Finish with a sprinkle of grated Parmesan.

Bake for 30 minutes, or until the tops of the cannelloni are golden and bubbling.

Basil-Walnut Pesto

Pesto made with walnuts (instead of pine nuts) has an earthier autumnal flavor. Many recipes suggest blending pesto in a food processor, but by chopping you get a much more interesting and authentic texture, including tiny nibs of toasted walnuts. A sleek, single-blade mezzaluna is perfect for this job; it makes the chopping so effortless. Yes, a boring old knife will do the same job, but less pleasurably! For a real feast of autumnal flavors, serve this with spaghetti and sautéed leeks.

Makes 1 cup

$\frac{1}{3}$ **cup (40 grams) walnut pieces**

2 garlic cloves

A handful of fresh basil leaves

$\frac{1}{4}$ **cup (30 grams) freshly grated Parmesan cheese**

4 or 5 tablespoons olive oil

Fine sea salt and freshly ground pepper

Preheat the broiler. Spread the walnuts on a rimmed baking sheet and place under the broiler for 2 to 3 minutes, watching carefully, until they begin to smell fragrant and toasty. Transfer to a chopping board with the garlic and start chopping. Gradually add the basil leaves and keep chopping until the ingredients begin to hold together in a paste.

Transfer to a bowl and add the Parmesan. Add the olive oil and stir to yield a thick paste. Season to taste with salt and pepper.

Acorn Squash and Chorizo Risotto

Served inside the squash skins, every forkful is a delicious combination of paprika-spiced risotto and smooth, sweet winter squash.

Serves 4

2 acorn squash (about 1 pound or 450 grams each)

4 tablespoons olive oil, divided

Sea salt and freshly ground pepper

7 ounces (200 grams) dry-cured Spanish chorizo, chopped into $1/2$-inch pieces

2 medium onions, chopped

$1 1/2$ cups (350 grams) Aborio rice

1 cup (200 milliliters) dry white wine

$4 1/2$ cups (1 liter) vegetable stock, heated and kept warm

$1/2$ cup (80 grams) grated Parmesan

A few fresh basil leaves, for serving

....

Preheat oven to 375°F (190°C).

Cut each squash in half lengthwise and scoop out the seeds. Brush the insides with 1 tablespoon of the olive oil, season with salt and pepper, and place cut-side down in a baking dish. Bake for about 45 minutes, until very tender. Test by piercing with the tip of a knife. Turn the oven off. Invert the squashes onto a serving dish. Scoop a large spoonful of flesh from each one, coarsely chop, and reserve in a bowl. Cover the roasted squash halves with foil and return to the oven to keep warm.

Heat the remaining 3 tablespoons olive oil in a large skillet over medium-low heat. Add the chorizo and the onions and sauté for 3 to 4 minutes, until the onions soften and the chorizo oozes spicy orange oil.

Add the rice, stirring for a minute until all the grains are coated with the oil. Add the wine, increase the heat slightly, and cook, stirring until all the wine has been absorbed. Add the stock a ladleful at a time, stirring regularly and waiting until each addition has been absorbed before adding any more.

Begin testing the rice after 15 minutes; the grains should be tender, but just slightly al dente, and the overall texture creamy, not dry. You may not need to add all the stock. Stir in the Parmesan and the chopped squash, and season with salt and pepper.

Spoon the risotto into the reserved baked squash halves and scatter over a few torn basil leaves. Serve hot.

Pork with Spiced Plums

Ripe plums sit like a blanket on top of the pork chops, keeping them succulent as they simmer in red wine and spices. Serve this with Aromatic Basil Rice (page 180).

Serves 4

4 boneless pork loin chops (about 2 pounds or 1 kilogram)

2 tablespoons balsamic vinegar

3 tablespoons butter, divided

1 medium onion, thinly sliced

1 pound (400 grams) red or purple plums (about 8),

    pitted and quartered

2 tablespoons granulated sugar

1¼ cups (300 milliliters) light red wine, such as Sangiovese,

    Chianti, or Burgundy

1 teaspoon Chinese 5-spice powder

Fine sea salt and freshly ground pepper

. . . .

Preheat the oven to 375°F (190°C).

Arrange the pork chops in a single layer in a wide, ovenproof dish. Pour the vinegar over the chops, coating them evenly, and leave to marinate for 30 minutes.

Melt 2 tablespoons of butter in a large skillet over medium-high heat. Brown the pork chops for a couple of minutes on both sides, in batches if necessary, then return to the ovenproof dish.

Reduce the heat to medium-low and melt the remaining tablespoon butter in the skillet. Add the onion and sauté for 5 minutes, until softened. Add the plums and the sugar and sauté for 5 minutes, stirring regularly with a spatula. Remove from the heat and spoon over the pork chops.

Pour the red wine into the skillet, add the 5-spice powder and salt and pepper, and bring to a boil, scraping the bottom of the pan to incorporate any browned bits. Allow the wine to reduce slightly, and carefully pour over the pork.

Cover the dish securely with a sheet of aluminum foil and cook in the oven for 25 minutes, until the chops are cooked through.

Transfer the pork to a warm serving dish. Pour the juices into a skillet over medium-high heat and reduce for a couple of minutes until thick and glossy. Drizzle over the pork and serve.

Aromatic Basil Rice

I grow green and purple basil in the greenhouse, bordering the tomato plants. When I pick the tomatoes, I feast on deep lungfuls of the aroma released by brushing against the basil leaves. Inspired, I always bring a bunch of basil back to the house. It's delicious torn and strewn into fluffy plain boiled rice.

Serves 4

1 cup (220 grams) basmati rice

Fine sea salt

A handful of fresh basil leaves, torn into small pieces

Fill a large saucepan with 8 cups (1.9 liters) of cold water. Add the rice and a teaspoon of salt and leave to soak for 30 minutes.

Bring the pan of water to a boil over medium heat, stir once, then reduce the heat to the lowest setting and leave the rice to cook for 7 or 8 minutes. Towards the end of the cooking time, check the rice for doneness. Each grain should be just cooked through, with no hard white center; if the rice overcooks, the grains will become soggy, and bend in a crescent shape. Pay attention! Take the pot off the heat and drain the rice immediately.

Stir in the torn basil and check the seasoning, adding more salt if necessary. Transfer to a warmed serving dish.

Chicken with
Apple-Cardamom Stuffing

The fruitiness of the autumnal stuffing is delicious with tender chicken and a whisper of salty dried ham. Cutting the chicken into slices reveals the stuffing. This is a great dish for entertaining, as it can be prepared well in advance, which will allow the flavors to mingle, then cooked just before serving.

Serves 4

8 cardamom pods

⅓ cup (50 grams) pine nuts

2 medium dessert apples (such as Jonagold
    or Golden Delicious), peeled, cored, and grated

⅓ cup (50 grams) raisins

¾ cup (50 grams) fresh breadcrumbs

2 teaspoons honey

Sea salt and freshly ground pepper

4 boneless, skinless, chicken breasts

4 slices prosciutto

Olive oil for drizzling

Preheat the oven to 375°F (190°C).

Lay a sheet of aluminum foil large enough to envelope all the chicken breasts on an ovenproof baking dish.

Split the cardamom pods to extract the seeds. Discard the pods, then grind the seeds in a mortar and pestle, or in a spice grinder.

Set a small dry skillet over medium heat, add the pine nuts, and toast for a couple of minutes until they turn golden. Transfer to a large bowl. Add the ground cardamon, grated apple, raisins, breadcrumbs, honey,

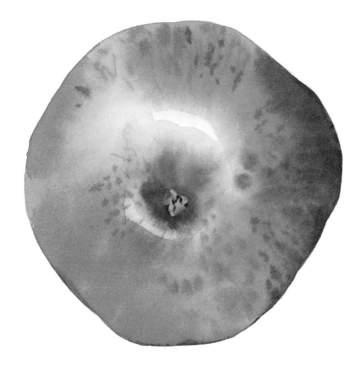

and salt and pepper; mix thoroughly. Go easy on the salt, as the prosciutto will add saltiness.

Place the chicken breasts on a work surface. Using a sharp knife, slice each one horizontally without cutting all the way through, making a pocket. Divide the stuffing among the 4 pockets. Wrap a slice of prosciutto around each fillet, to hold it together, and place on the prepared foil. Drizzle the chicken with a little olive oil then seal the fillets in a foil parcel.

Bake for 20 minutes, then open the foil and return to the oven for a further 5 minutes. When cooked, the chicken should feel firm to the touch. Let the chicken rest for 5 minutes before serving.

To serve, cut each chicken breast crosswise into 1½-inch-thick slices, and lay them on their side on warmed plates.

Apple Cake

This is a fantastically easy cake to whip up for dessert when an apple windfall needs immediate attention. It is best served while still warm from the oven, dusted with confectioners' sugar.

Makes one 8-inch cake

3 large eggs

6 tablespoons (75 grams) castor (superfine) sugar

6 tablespoons (75 grams) unsalted butter, melted

3 medium-size apples (choose a tart variety that holds its shape when cooked, such as Granny Smith), peeled, cored, and cut into thin 1/4-inch slices

1 1/4 cups (150 grams) self-rising flour

2 teaspoons baking powder

Preheat oven to 350°F (180°C). Grease an 8-inch round cake pan and line the bottom with parchment paper.

Using an electric mixer, beat together the eggs and sugar until pale and fluffy. Add the melted butter and mix well. Add the apple slices and stir gently with a spoon to coat them with the batter. Sift the flour and baking powder into the apple batter, stirring just to combine. Pour the batter into the prepared cake pan. Bake until the top is golden brown and the center of the cake is springy to the touch, about 30 minutes.

Pear and Almond Cake

A lovely moist and fragrant cake, perfect for afternoon tea today, tomorrow and the next day. It keeps well, if it lasts that long.

Makes one 8 x 4-inch loaf

7 tablespoons (100 grams) butter

½ cup (125 grams) caster (superfine) sugar

2 large eggs, lightly beaten

3 tablespoons cream cheese, at room temperature

1 medium-sized crisp pear, peeled, cored, and grated, (about ½ cup, or 150 grams)

½ cup (50 grams) almond meal (substitute raw almonds ground in a food processor to a fine powder)

1 cup (100 grams) self-rising flour, sifted

Preheat oven to 325°F (170°C).

Grease and line an 8 x 4-inch loaf pan with parchment paper.

Cream the butter and sugar with an electric mixer until pale and fluffy. Beat in the eggs one at a time, adding a tablespoon of the flour if the mixture curdles. Beat in the cream cheese and the pear, then gradually fold in the flour and the almond meal. Pour the batter into the prepared loaf pan.

Bake for about 55 minutes, until a skewer inserted into the center comes out clean.

Butternut Squash and Pumpkin Seed Loaf

Squash in disguise, this lovely, moist teatime loaf might even fool the most ardent squash hater: my husband! Use a smaller loaf pan (4 x 6-inch) for this bread.

Makes 1 loaf

1 large egg

½ **cup (100 grams) castor (superfine) sugar**

¼ **cup (50 milliliters) sunflower oil or other neutral oil**

2 ½ **ounces (75 grams) winter squash (any variety), peeled if necessary and coarsely grated**

½ **cup (75 grams) whole wheat flour**

½ **teaspoon baking powder**

1 teaspoon apple pie spice, or a combination of ground cinnamon, ginger, and allspice

1 tablespoon demerara-style raw sugar, for sprinkling

1 tablespoon pumpkin seeds

Preheat oven to 350°F (180°C). Grease a 4 x 6-inch loaf pan and line the bottom with parchment paper.

Using an electric mixer, beat together the egg and sugar in a mixing bowl until pale and fluffy, about 3 minutes. Add the oil and beat to combine. Stir in the grated squash, then gently fold in the flour, baking powder, and spice.

Pour into the prepared pan and sprinkle with the demerara sugar and the pumpkin seeds.

Bake for 30 to 40 minutes, or until a skewer inserted in the center comes out clean. Cool on a wire rack.

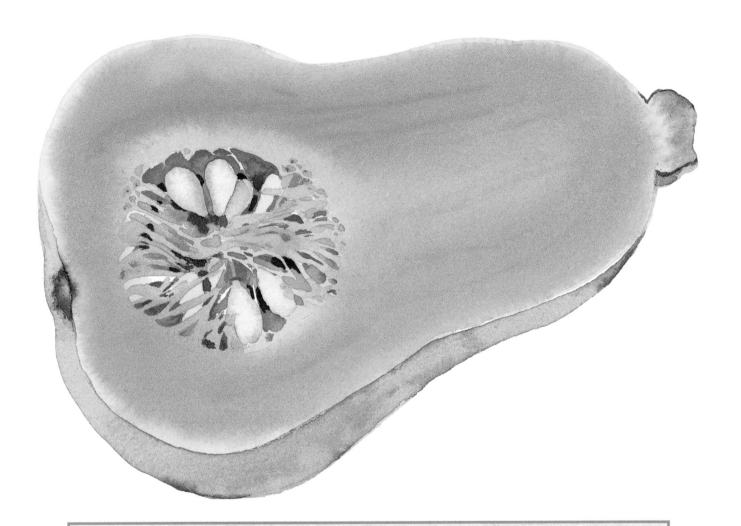

Butternut Squash

Squashes seem to fall into the love-it-or-hate-it category: they can be alternately rich, sweet, and creamy or bland, textureless, and far too prolific. When they're good, I love them. They keep for months and are packed with vitamin C, so the more recipes on hand, the better.

Hot Cross Kebabs

The origin of this recipe was a hastily engineered dessert of leftover hot cross buns and a bowl of freshly picked plums. As a rule, anything served on a stick generates an extra level of expectation in our house, and this yummy treat of warm, juicy spiced plums and toasty currant croutons did not disappoint. The next time I experimented, I used the Currant Tea Loaf (page 190). Feel free to use hot cross buns or teacakes from the bakery for a quick and easy option.

Serves 4

8 large plums (mixed varieties will be prettier if you
   have them)

¼ cup (60 milliliters) maple syrup

½ teaspoon freshly grated nutmeg

½ teaspoon ground ginger

2 thick slices Currant Tea Loaf (page 190) or 2 hot cross buns

¼ cup (60 milliliters) sunflower oil

Plain Greek-style yogurt, for serving

Preheat the oven to 400°F (200°C). Line a baking sheet with parchment paper.

Halve the plums to remove the stones, and then quarter the flesh. Combine the plum quarters in a large bowl with the maple syrup and the spices, and stir to coat evenly.

Cut each slice of currant loaf into 8 cubes, then toss the chunks in another large bowl with the sunflower oil. Thread the pieces of plum and currant loaf on 4 metal skewers, alternating between 2 pieces of fruit and 1 piece of bread.

Place the skewers on the prepared baking sheet, drizzle over any remaining spiced maple syrup, and bake for 10 minutes, turning once, until the plums look juicy and the bread is golden-brown. Allow to cool slightly.

Serve the kebabs, scraping every last drop of gooey syrup off the parchment, with a dollop of creamy Greek-style yogurt.

Currant Tea Loaf

A delicious loaf containing plump currants soaked in tea is perfect for a light supper, toasted and spread with butter.

Makes 1 loaf

⅓ cup (50 grams) currants

6 ounces (175 milliliters) hot rooibos tea (or any nice amber-colored tea)

2 cups (250 grams) unbleached white bread flour

1½ tablespoons unsalted butter

1 teaspoon active dry yeast (from ¼-ounce packet)

2 tablespoons castor (superfine) sugar, plus more for sprinkling on top

Pinch fine sea salt

2 tablespoons milk, for brushing on top

Add the currants to the hot tea and set aside to soak; allow the tea to cool to lukewarm.

In a large bowl, rub the butter into the flour with your fingers. When it resembles coarse breadcrumbs, make a well in the center and add the yeast, sugar, and salt. Check the temperature of the tea with an instant-read thermometer; if it is too hot it will kill the yeast. When lukewarm (110°F or 45°C), pour the tea into the well in the flour along with the currants. Mix with a spoon to form a dough, then knead on a floured work surface for 2 to 3 minutes, or until the dough is silky-smooth and elastic and no longer sticks to the work surface. Pop the dough back into the mixing bowl, cover with a damp cloth and leave in a warm place to rise until doubled in bulk, about 1 hour.

Grease an 8 x 4-inch loaf pan and set aside.

When the dough has doubled in bulk, return it to the floured board and knead again for a few seconds, just enough to release the air. Shape it to fit into the prepared loaf pan and leave to rise again, covered

loosely with a damp cloth in a warm place, until it is has risen just above the top of the pan. It should take about half an hour, depending on the temperature of the room. The more bread you bake, the better you'll get at judging.

Meanwhile, preheat the oven to 375°F (190°C). When the dough has risen to just above the top of the pan, brush the top with milk and sprinkle with a little sugar, then bake for 25 minutes. Remove from the pan, when cooked the base should sound hollow when tapped. Cool on a wire rack.

Blackberry and Almond Scrunchies

These pretty little parcels of ripe blackberries and melting marzipan encased in layers of wafer-thin pastry are the perfect juicy-chewy-crispy combination.

Serves 4

8 sheets fresh or frozen thawed phyllo pastry

5 tablespoons (75 grams) melted unsalted butter

½ pint (7 ounces or 200 grams) blackberries

5 ounces (150 grams) marzipan, cut into small cubes

2 tablespoons castor (superfine) sugar

Preheat oven to 400°F (200°C). Grease a large baking sheet.

On a work surface, quarter each phyllo sheet to yield a total of 32 squares. Keep the stack of phyllo squares covered with a damp cloth or piece of plastic wrap to prevent them from drying out. Lay the first sheet on your work surface and brush with some of the melted butter. Place a second sheet on top of the first, shifted 45 degrees, to create an 8-pointed star. Brush with butter and repeat the process with layers 3 and 4, continuing to slightly rotate each layer. In the center of your phyllo, place 5 or 6 blackberries, depending on size, and 3 or 4 pieces of marzipan. Sprinkle with a teaspoon of sugar. This is not an exact science but there should be enough pastry surrounding the fruit to be able to lift up the edges by the corners and twist them together to make a little frilly-topped bundle. Imagine twisting a handful of candy in the corner of a paper bag and you're halfway there. If you are overly generous with the blackberries, the bundles will leak sticky fruit juice and the phyllo will tear from the weight. Brush the tops with the remainder of the melted butter. You should have 8 parcels in total.

Spread the parcels out on the prepared baking sheet and bake for 10 minutes. They are delicious warm from the oven and served with whipped cream.

Blackberry and Apple Ice Cream

This has all the flavor of traditional blackberry and apple pie with custard, but under a more summery guise. Choose an apple variety that disintegrates well when cooked, such as McIntosh. Serve with fresh blackberries and Crisp Butter Biscuits (page 49).

Makes 1 quart (1 liter)

1 recipe Basic Ice Cream (page 119)

1 cup (250 milliliters) heavy whipping cream (double cream)

2 dessert apples (about 8 ounces or 250 grams peeled weight),

peeled, cored, and sliced

4 ounces (125 grams) blackberries

2 tablespoons (25 grams) castor (superfine) sugar

Make the Basic Ice Cream up to the point of freezing it. When it has cooled slightly, stir in the cream and refrigerate.

Set a small pot over a medium heat, and cook the apples in a couple of tablespoons of water until they are soft and beginning to disintegrate. Transfer the apples to a blender or food processor and blend until they are perfectly smooth. Stir into the unfrozen ice cream.

Pour the custard mixture into your ice cream maker and freeze according to manufacturer's directions.

Meanwhile, combine the blackberries and the sugar in the blender and purée. Strain through a fine mesh sieve to extract the seeds. Stir the blackberry syrup into the finished ice cream, just enough to retain deep purple swirls through the vanilla.

Baked Orchard Fruits

This simple dessert is a medley of rich, syrupy fruits slowly softened in the oven to intensify their flavor. It is the sort of dish you can pop in the oven when you're busy with something else, especially if you have heavily laden fruit trees in the garden. Exact weights are not vital here: just get similar quantities of each fruit. Delicious served with vanilla custard or Greek yogurt, and Best Walnut Biscuits (page 200).

Serves 4

2 dessert apples, preferably a variety that keeps its shape when cooked, such as Jonagold

2 pears

4 plums (purple or red)

6 tablespoons (80 grams) dark brown muscovado sugar or any packed dark brown sugar

2 teaspoons apple pie spice, or a combination of ground cinnamon, ginger, and allspice

6 cardamom pods, seeds finely ground in a spice grinder or mortar and pestle

Juice of 1 lemon

Preheat oven to 300°F (150°C).

Peel and core the apples and the pears, and cut into ½-inch slices. Halve the plums, remove the pits, and quarter. Arrange all the fruit in a single layer in the bottom of a large, ovenproof baking dish.

Sprinkle the fruit with the sugar, spice, and cardamom, tossing to coat evenly, then drizzle the lemon juice over the top. Cover tightly with a sheet of aluminum foil and bake for 30 minutes, until the fruit is soft and gives off a pool of syrup.

Transfer to a serving bowl, and serve just slightly warm.

Savory Fennel-Seed Oat Biscuits

These biscuits are slightly sweet and are a delicious accompaniment to a cheese course. A traditional aid to digestion, the fennel seeds may even compensate for over-indulgence! Try these dipped into the Herbed Mousse (page 16) or Chile and Cream Cheese Dip (page 136), along with a cool glass of something nice.

Makes 20 biscuits

2 teaspoons fennel seeds

1 cup (100 grams) all-purpose flour

½ teaspoon fine sea salt

1½ cups (100 grams) rolled oats

¼ cup (50 grams) castor (superfine) sugar

5 tablespoons (70 grams) unsalted butter, cut into small pieces

1 large egg, beaten

. . . .

Preheat oven to 350° F (180°C). Line a baking sheet with parchment paper.

Set a small, dry pan over medium heat, add the fennel seeds, and toast for a couple of minutes until they are fragrant. Set aside.

Combine the flour, salt, oats, and sugar in a large mixing bowl, stir just to combine, and rub in the butter with your fingers until the mixture resembles coarse breadcrumbs. Add the toasted fennel seeds and the egg and mix with a spoon to form a dough. (If the egg is not sufficient to bind the mixture, add a tiny splash of milk.)

Roll the dough out on a floured board to about ⅛-inch thick. Use a biscuit cutter to cut into circles and

arrange them on the prepared baking sheet; they can be quite close together as they won't spread. Bake for 15 minutes, until the edges are just turning golden, but don't overbake. Cool on a wire rack and store at room temperature in an airtight container, for up to 3 weeks.

Poppy Seed Crackers

After you've slaved away preparing for a dinner party, your guests will forgive you for shaking crackers out of a package for the cheese course. However, these easy-to-make crackers taste and look so fantastic, can be made in advance, and will keep for ages in an airtight tin—so no excuses! Depending on the local laws governing the propagation of poppies, you may need to resort to the supermarket rather than shaking the seeds out of those lovely bulbous seed heads in the flower garden.

Makes about 3 dozen

2 teaspoons poppy seeds

1 ½ cups (200 grams) all-purpose flour

½ teaspoon fine sea salt

2 tablespoons olive oil

½ cup (100 milliliters) ice water

Preheat the oven to 350ºF (180ºC). Line a large baking sheet with parchment paper.

Set a small, heavy skillet over medium-low heat and toast the poppy seeds for 2 to 3 minutes, until they are just beginning to smell fragrant. Remove the pan from the heat and set the seeds aside.

Combine the flour and salt in a large mixing bowl and make a well in the center. Stir in the oil, poppy seeds, and cold water by tablespoonfuls just until the dough holds together. Knead briefly to make a smooth dough.

Transfer the dough to a floured board, and using half the dough at a time roll it out literally as thin as you can, almost translucent. If they are too thick they will have the texture of cardboard. The dough should hold together well but if you're concerned about it sticking to the board or the rolling pin, roll it between two large sheets of waxed paper or parchment paper. Cut the dough into squares of roughly 2 ½ inches, and prick each in the center with the tines of a fork. (You could also use a round cookie cutter, but dividing into squares eliminates having to re-roll the leftovers.)

Place the squares of dough on the prepared baking sheet quite close together, and bake for 10 minutes, or until golden. They will bubble and warp while baking, which is completely acceptable, desirable even! Cool on a wire rack and store at room temperature in an airtight container, for up to 3 weeks.

Best Walnut Biscuits

Anticipating a crop of walnuts from our fledgling nut grove, I have adapted a classic Shrewsbury biscuit dough to include crispy, caramelized walnuts. Pay attention when roasting the walnuts: a momentary loss of concentration can quickly result in an acrid, smoking skillet. Not to mention the waste of an entire crop of walnuts! Perfection on their own with a cup of tea, or for dessert with Baked Orchard Fruits (page 195).

Makes 15 biscuits

CARAMELIZED WALNUTS

1 tablespoon sunflower oil or other neutral oil

½ cup (50 grams) chopped walnuts

1 tablespoon balsamic vinegar

½ teaspoon freshly ground pepper

2 tablespoons light brown muscovado sugar or packed light brown sugar

BISCUITS

½ cup (100 grams) castor (superfine) sugar, plus extra for sprinkling

½ cup (115 grams) butter

1 egg yolk

1¾ cups (175 grams) all-purpose flour

....

Preheat oven to 350°F (180°C). Line a large baking sheet with parchment paper. Spread additional parchment paper on a work surface.

For the walnuts: Heat the oil in a skillet over medium heat. Add the walnuts, vinegar, and pepper, and cook, stirring frequently, for 3 to 4 minutes until the walnuts just begin to smell toasty. Add the sugar and continue to stir to keep the nuts from sticking together. With a watchful eye, cook for 2 minutes or until the sugar just begins to melt, then immediately spread the nuts on the sheet of parchment paper to cool.

For the biscuits: Combine the castor sugar and butter in a mixing bowl, and beat with an electric mixer until pale and fluffy. Beat in the egg yolk, then stir in the flour and caramelized walnuts with a metal spoon to make a stiff paste.

Turn the dough out onto a floured board and knead briefly, then roll out to about ¼-inch thick. Use a 2½- or 3-inch cookie cutter to cut out about 15 circles. Transfer them to the prepared baking sheet and bake for about 15 minutes, until just barely golden. Lightly sprinkle with castor sugar while still hot, then transfer to a wire cooling rack to cool completely.

Pear and Walnut Focaccia

A slightly sweet, beautifully soft bread, studded with spiced pear and toasted walnuts. Delicious with salad and crumbly cheeses.

Serves 8

TOPPING

2 tablespoons butter

2 firm pears, peeled cored and chopped into ¾-inch chunks

½ cup (40 grams) walnuts, roughly chopped

1 tablespoon muscovado sugar

Freshly grated nutmeg

Coarse sea salt and freshly ground pepper

BREAD

1 recipe Basic Bread dough (omit the salt and double the sugar, and allow to rise once until doubled in bulk, page 54)

1 large egg

1 ½ tablespoons (25 grams) butter chopped into small pieces

For the topping: Melt the butter in a skillet over medium-high heat, add the pears, walnuts, and sugar, and cook for three or four minutes tossing regularly until the sugar begins to caramelize. Season with plenty of nutmeg, salt, and pepper. Set aside to cool.

For the bread: Grease a 12 x 8-inch baking sheet. Turn the risen dough out onto a floured board, make a well in the center, and crack the egg into the hollow. Bring the edges of the dough into the center, gradually kneading in the egg. This is meant to be a sticky job; egg will ooze everywhere. Don't be tempted to add more flour as this will make the bread denser; just persevere. Wash and flour your hands halfway through if necessary. Eventually, when the egg is fully incorporated the dough should be very soft and smooth.

Place the dough on the prepared baking sheet, spreading it with your fingers until it covers the sheet. Leave in a warm place to rise for about 30 minutes, covered with a damp cloth.

Preheat the oven to 450°F (240°C).

When the dough looks puffy and has doubled in size, sprinkle the pear and walnuts evenly over the top, pressing the chunks of pear into the dough with your fingers. Dot with the pieces of butter.

Bake for 15 minutes, or until firm and golden-brown. Cool on a wire rack, or best of all, devour while still warm.

Crabapple and Herb Jelly

If you don't have crabapples in the garden, look out for them growing wild, or substitute sour cooking apples. (The jelly won't set if you use a sweet apple.) You may also find them at some farmer's markets in season. The beauty of this recipe is that you can use the crabapples whole and their crimson skins give the jelly a translucent peachy glow. This versatile jelly is great with roast lamb or pork—a spoonful can transform a gravy—and it's good with crumbly cheeses.

Makes four 12-ounce (340 gram) jars

6 pounds (3 kilograms) crabapples, or sour cooking apples

Granulated sugar

Juice of 1 lemon

4 cloves

Large bunch of mint, tied in a bundle, plus 6 tablespoons finely chopped fresh mint

HERB JELLY

Prepare four 12-ounce glass canning jars by washing and sterilizing them. (See page 61 for instructions.)

Wash the apples and remove any blemishes. Leave crabapples whole; cooking apples should be cut into quarters. Put apples in a large, heavy stockpot with enough water to not quite cover the apples. Bring to a boil over high heat, then reduce the heat to medium-low and simmer for about 30 minutes, until the fruit is soft and falling apart. Remove from the heat and set aside.

Set a large mesh strainer over a bowl big enough to hold all the fruit and line with cheesecloth or a clean kitchen towel, or use a jelly bag. Strain the fruit overnight, until all the juice has been extracted from the seeds and pulp. Don't squeeze the pulp; in this instance, you want to keep the jelly clear so you can see the herbs suspended in it.

When the bag has stopped dripping, discard the pulp. Measure the juice and return it to the large pot. Add 2 ½ cups (500 grams) granulated sugar per 1 pint (500 milliliters) of juice. Heat gently over medium-low heat, stirring until the sugar dissolves. Add the lemon juice, cloves, and the tied bunch of mint. Increase the heat to medium and boil steadily for about 30 minutes, or until setting point is reached. You can use a thermometer (most jellies and jams will set at 220°F or 105°C), or spoon a blob of the jelly onto a cold saucer, place the saucer in the freezer for 1 to 2 minutes, then remove it and try pushing the jelly with your finger. If the surface has begun to form a skin, it will wrinkle when you push it, and it's ready for jarring. If it hasn't begun to form a skin, continue to cook for another 2 to 3 minutes, and test again. You may need to repeat this test a few times.

Remove the cloves and bunch of mint, and stir in the chopped mint. Spoon the jelly into the sterilized glass jars. Screw on the metal lids while the jelly is still hot, and allow to cool on the counter. The jelly will keep, unopened, in a cool, dry place for 1 year or opened, in the refrigerator, for 6 months.

Raspberry Vinegar

Vinegar has long been used as a household cleaner. It will remove a scummy ring from the bath, red wine from the carpet, and blast through the blackened base of a burnt saucepan. As a child, the first tickle of a sore throat was warded off with a hot mug of my mother's raspberry vinegar. Not only did I love this steaming, fruity concoction, but I'm sure it had the bacteria in my throat reeling. Not limited to medicinal purposes, fruit vinegars are great as a base for salad dressings. Raspberry is my favorite fruit to use, but any sharp fruit can be substituted; I've made this with blackberries, red currants, and black currants.

Makes about 4 pints (1.9 liters)

2 pounds (900 grams) raspberries

2 pints (950 milliliters) white distilled vinegar

Granulated sugar, as needed

Prepare enough glass bottles with securely fitting lids to hold 4 pints of liquid by washing and sterilizing them. (See page 61 for instructions.)

Combine the raspberries and vinegar in a large bowl and leave for 2 to 3 days, stirring occasionally. The raspberries will break down.

Set a fine mesh sieve over a large measuring glass and strain the vinegar, pressing the pulp with the back of a wooden spoon to extract as much juice as possible.

Measure the liquid, then combine the juice in a large heavy stockpot with 1¼ cups (225 grams) sugar per 2 cups (500 milliliters) of liquid. Set over medium heat, gently stirring until the sugar has dissolved, then boil

for 10 minutes until it becomes slightly syrupy. Pour into the warm sterilized bottles and seal. The vinegar

will keep for years in a cool, dark pantry.

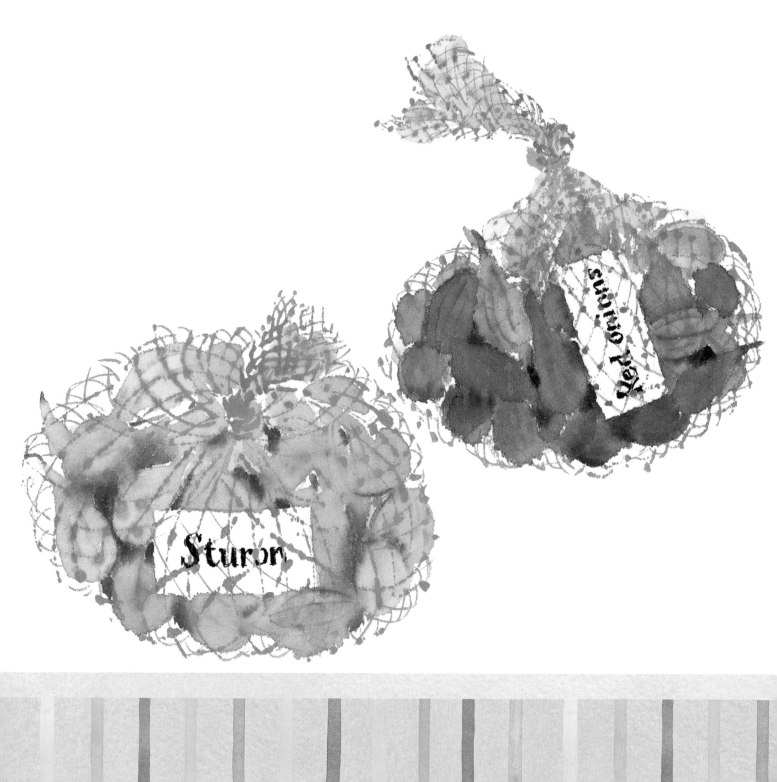

Onion Marmalade

A thick, oniony sludge really, with a hint of sweet and sour, this number-one standby is good to have in the fridge for eating with cheese, to spice up sauces, and to slather on sausages. Make it with regular or red onions, or a mix of both.

Makes two 12-ounce (340 gram) jars

1 tablespoon olive oil

1 tablespoon chile oil

2 pounds (1 kilogram) onions, diced

½ cup (100 grams) packed light brown sugar

2 tablespoons balsamic vinegar

2 tablespoons Marsala or sweet sherry

Pinch of salt

Prepare two 12-ounce glass canning jars by washing and sterilizing them. (See page 61 for instructions.)

Heat the oils in a wide, heavy pot over medium heat, add the onions, and sauté gently until soft. Add the sugar, stirring until it has dissolved. Add the vinegar and sherry; cover with a lid and simmer over a very low heat, for 1 ½ hours. Remove the lid towards the end of the cooking time and stir frequently until it has reduced to a lovely sticky marmalade. Season with salt and remove from the heat.

Spoon into the sterilized glass jars. Screw on the metal lids while still hot, and allow to cool on the counter. The jam will keep, unopened, in a cool dry place for 2 months or opened, in the refrigerator, for 1 month.

Blackberry Jelly

This preserve embodies the turning of the seasons when the haze of summer is eclipsed by dewy mornings: it's sweet and sharp with a mellow note. Blackberries are very seedy so I prefer to make a strained jelly, which is delicious with scones, cakes, and of course, cream.

Makes five 12-ounce (340 gram) jars

2 pounds (1 kilogram) blackberries, washed

Juice of 2 lemons

Granulated sugar, as needed

Prepare five 12-ounce glass canning jars by washing and sterilizing them. (See page 61 for instructions.)

Put the blackberries in a large, heavy pot along with about ½ cup (100 milliliters) water. Simmer gently over medium heat until tender. As the berries soften, crush them with a potato masher or with a wooden spoon against the side of the pot. When they have broken down almost completely, after about 40 minutes, remove the pot from the heat.

Set a large mesh strainer over a bowl big enough to hold all the berries. Line the strainer with cheesecloth or a clean kitchen towel, or use a jelly bag. Strain the blackberries overnight, until all the juice has been extracted from the seeds and pulp. If you want a clear jelly, don't crush the fruit pulp to release more juice; if you don't mind it slightly cloudy (I don't) and want maximum yield (I do), then press as much juice as you can out of the fruit.

Measure the blackberry juice and return it to the pot with the lemon juice over medium-low heat. Add 2½ cups (450 grams) sugar per pint (450 milliliters) of juice. Heat slowly, stirring until the sugar has dissolved, then increase the heat and boil rapidly until setting point is reached. You can use a thermometer (most jellies and jams will set at 220°F (105°C), or test it for setting by spooning a small blob of jam onto a cold saucer. Place the saucer in the freezer for 1 to 2 minutes, then remove it and try pushing the jam with your finger. If the surface wrinkles, it's ready. If it hasn't begun to form a skin, continue to cook for another 2 to 3 minutes, and test again. You may need to repeat this test a few times.

Remove the pan from the heat as soon as setting point has been reached. Spoon the jelly into the sterilized glass jars. Screw on the metal lids while the jelly is still hot, and allow to cool on the counter. The jam will keep, unopened, in a cool, dry place for 1 year or opened, in the refrigerator, for 4 months.

Blackberries

In late summer I get very excited about the wild blackberries that festoon the hedges around where I live. Each year, I watch the pink blossoms unfurl, then the berries redden and ripen into perfectly glossy, deep purple jewels. Perhaps my obsession is all the greater for never having to tend to their needs. Starting with the south-facing branches, I pick my way through a long season of pies, jams, jellies, flavored vinegar, and best of all, a handful of fresh berries for breakfast.

Quince Paste

Membrillo, or quince paste, is a Spanish delicacy: quince, simmered slowly with sugar until it reduces to a thick, dense jelly, is eaten in dabs with hard Manchego cheese. It's delicious and you don't even need to peel or core the fruit, so when my husband planted our orchard, there had to be a quince tree.

Makes three 12-ounce (340 gram) jars

2 pounds (1 kilogram) quinces

Juice of ½ lemon

Granulated sugar

Olive oil

Prepare three 12-ounce glass canning jars by washing and sterilizing them. (See page 61 for instructions.)

Coarsely chop the whole fruit, discarding any blemishes. Put the chopped quinces in a large pot with enough water to just cover. Bring to a light boil over low heat and simmer very slowly with the lid on until the fruit is soft. This will take 2 to 3 hours, but don't try to hurry it; long cooking brings out the gorgeous deep pink color of the fruit. Add a little water if the pulp is becoming too dry.

Drain the pulp and cool slightly, and either pummel it with a potato masher and pass it through a coarse sieve, or blend it to a paste in a food processor, and then force it through a sieve.

Weigh the paste on a kitchen scale, and combine it in a large, heavy pot with the same weight of sugar. Add the lemon juice and bring to a gentle simmer over low heat. Simmer, stirring frequently, until the sugar has dissolved. Continue to simmer very gently for about 2 hours, until the paste is really thick. You should be able to see the bottom of the pan when you drag a spoon through the paste. Don't wander off and forget about it though; stir regularly to make sure it is not burning on the bottom of the pan.

Wipe the insides of the sterilized jars with a piece of lightly oiled kitchen towel. Spoon the paste into the oiled sterilized glass jars. Screw on the metal lids while the paste is still hot, and allow to cool on the counter. The paste will keep, unopened, in a cool, dry place for 2 years or opened, in the refrigerator, for 6 months.

Quince

My father's quince tree is his pride and joy; each blossom is a twirl of pink and white candy stripe as it unfurls, begging you to pry it open, and the leaves are downy to the touch. The ripe fruits exude such an exotic spiced-apple perfume that a bowl full will scent the whole house. They are, however, the bane of my mother's life: as quinces are inedible raw and rock-hard, each quince-infused apple pie is a labor of love.

Winter

"Don't vegetate as you get older if you happen to live in the country. Some women are like cows but there is really no need to stagnate. Keep both brain and body on the move."

—Blanche Ebbutt, 1913

Winter can seem long and dark, and the ground is mostly wet

or frozen. At best, bare twigs scribble across clear blue skies; at worst, the day hardly wakes from a

monochromatic blur. I am forced to venture outside to scavenge for supper or to let the chickens out of their coop, grateful for a warm egg to cradle in my frozen hands, but I am happiest in the kitchen, kneading warm dough and simmering hearty soups.

The first hard frost in November reduces the dahlias to blackened, broken stems: time to cover them with sheep fleeces and black plastic for the winter. The parsnips, however, benefit from the cold weather: they sit tight in the ground, and become sweeter by the day. The last few will be saved for Christmas.

Just as we're beginning to run out of vegetables, my seed order rattles through the letterbox. I scrabble impatiently through the packets for something I can sow—now! Experience persuades me to restrain my enthusiasm and brave the frost instead to dig up some leeks for dinner. I am cheered by the sight of spiky rows of garlic and bright green broad bean shoots, cozy under their cloches.

It's the purple florets of sprouting broccoli that I look forward to most though: after a whole year of nurture, they shoot up succulent stems when the garden is at its bleakest.

Winter

Dishes and Starters

Cabbage with Roasted Garlic and Currants

Spinach Mashed Potatoes with a Hint of Garlic

Lemon-Garlic Oven Fries

Spicy Baked Parsnips

Root Vegetable Bake

Parsnip and Apple Fritters

Shredded Brussels Sprouts with Chorizo

Red Cabbage with Marmalade

Winter Coleslaw with Fennel and Pear

Onion and Celery Soup

Red Onion Yorkshire Puddings

Caramelized Onion Dumplings

Mains

Braised Beef with Chorizo and Celery

Root Vegetable Tarte Tatin

Mussels with Shallots and Parsley

Slow-Cooked Rabbit with Mustard and Thyme

Rabbit Risotto

Desserts

Apple-Ginger Meringue Cake

Black Currant Crumble Tarts

Black Currant and Almond-Baked Apple

Black Currant Mousse

Sundries

Orchard Chutney

Balsamic Pear and Beet Relish

Cabbage with Roasted Garlic and Currants

Combined with garlic and occasional fruity bites of dried currant, this is cabbage dressed up for a night out with its perfect partner, the potato. I've used savoy cabbage here, but any green cabbage will work well. The most important ingredient is freshness: look for a good heavy head with stiff, unwilted outer leaves. The cabbage cooks quickly, but you will need to allow 40 minutes for roasting the garlic, which can be prepared well ahead of time and kept in the fridge.

Serves 4

1 head garlic

2 teaspoons olive oil

2 tablespoons dry white wine

½ head savoy cabbage (about 1 pound or 450 grams)

1 tablespoon unsalted butter

½ cup (100 grams) currants

Pinch of freshly grated nutmeg

Fine sea salt and freshly ground pepper

Preheat oven to 375°F (190°C).

Slice about ¼ inch off the top of the garlic head, just far enough down to cut the tips off the individual cloves. Place the garlic on a square of foil large enough to encase the whole head and drizzle the cut surfaces with the oil and the wine. Wrap the foil tightly around the garlic, place in a small baking dish, and bake for about 40 minutes, until the garlic feels soft when squeezed. Unwrap partially, without letting the juices leak out, and let sit until cool enough to handle.

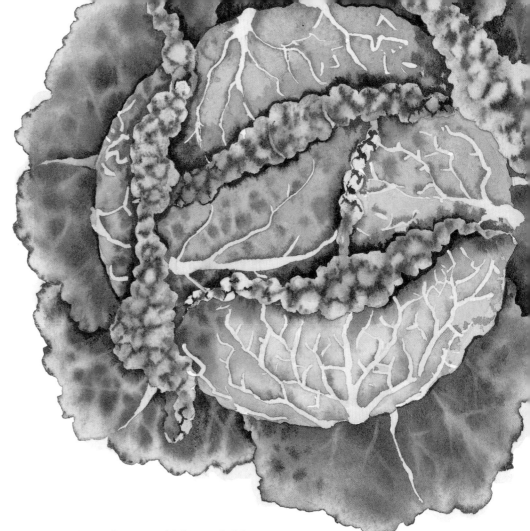

Slice the cabbage into ½-inch ribbons, discarding any thick woody bits.

Melt the butter in a skillet over low heat. Squeeze the roasted garlic out of the skins and add to the skillet, along with any collected garlic juices from the foil, and mash together with a fork. Add the cabbage, tossing it around in the butter. Sprinkle in the currants, then cover tightly and cook for 5 to 6 minutes. Shake the pan regularly to prevent sticking, adding a splash of water if necessary. The cabbage should be tender when pierced with a sharp knife, but not soggy. Add a pinch of freshly grated nutmeg and season to taste with salt and pepper.

Spinach Mashed Potatoes with a Hint of Garlic

Mashed potatoes must be the ultimate comfort food. Their undemanding taste and texture makes them the perfect host to entertain a spicier companion. Mustard or parsley work well as accompaniments, but for a sausage-and-mash dinner with steaming cabbage, roasted garlic is my favorite.

Serves 4

1 small head garlic

1 tablespoon olive oil

1 pound (450 grams) baking potatoes, such as Idaho or Yukon gold, peeled and quartered

¼ cup (50 milliliters) whole milk, heated and kept warm

2 tablespoons plus 1 teaspoon unsalted butter, divided, at room temperature

¼ cup (50 milliliters) whole milk, heated and kept warm

Fine sea salt and freshly ground pepper

½ pound (200 grams) spinach (substitute ½ cup thawed frozen spinach)

Preheat the oven to 350°F (180°C).

Cut a ¼-inch slice off the top of the garlic bulb to expose the tips of the cloves. Center the bulb on a square of aluminum foil large enough to wrap around it, and drizzle the olive oil over the bulb. Wrap the foil up tightly around the garlic and bake for about 40 minutes, until soft. After baking, vent the foil package and allow the garlic to cool.

Fill a pot with 1 inch of water. Place a steamer insert in the pot and bring the water to a boil. Alternatively, bring a large pot of water to boil.

Add the potatoes to the pot of water and steam or boil for about 15 minutes until they are soft and can be easily pierced with a knife.

Drain well and return the potatoes to the hot pan. Put the pan over a very low heat for about 30 seconds, just to evaporate any excess water. Shake the pot to keep the potatoes from sticking.

Squeeze the roasted garlic cloves out of their skins and add to the potatoes. Add the milk and 2 tablespoons of butter, and mash well with a potato masher or ricer. The latter will give a smoother texture. Season with salt and pepper.

Heat the remaining teaspoon of butter in a small skillet, and sauté the spinach until wilted and tender. Squeeze every last drop of moisture from the spinach then scatter onto the potato and stir in briefly, so you get lovely, deep green flecks. Serve in a warmed dish.

Lemon-Garlic Oven Fries

I first made these fries to go with our Friday night mussels (page 244). They are sturdy enough to dip into mayonnaise, and have just a tang of lemon and garlic.

Serves 4

3 pounds (1.2 kilograms) Yukon gold or Idaho potatoes

5 tablespoons sunflower (75 milliliters) oil or light olive oil

5 garlic cloves, minced

1 ½ lemons, cut into 8 segments

Coarse sea salt

Preheat oven to 450°F (230°C). Bring a large pot of water to boil over high heat.

Peel the potatoes and cut into ¾-inch-thick lengths. Add the potatoes to the boiling water and cook for about 4 to 5 minutes, until just softening at the edges. Drain well and return the potatoes to the pot over very low heat to evaporate any excess moisture. Keep shaking the pot to prevent the potatoes from sticking.

Combine the oil with the crushed garlic, and drizzle it over the potatoes. Turn them carefully to coat with the oil. Arrange the potatoes in a single layer on a couple of large baking sheets, and dot the lemon segments evenly between them. Sprinkle with coarse sea salt and cook for about 35 minutes, or until the fries are deep golden and have crispy edges and soft interiors. Turn at least once during cooking, to ensure even browning.

Serve with a big bowl of Mayonnaise (page 56) to dip into.

Spicy Baked Parsnips

This side dish lends a spicy Middle Eastern twist to straightforward roasted parsnips and goes well with succulent roast pork.

Serves 4

12 ounces (350 grams) root vegetables (parsnips and sweet potatoes work well together), peeled and cut into 2-inch chunks

3 tablespoons light olive oil, divided

2 teaspoons coriander seeds

2 teaspoons cumin seeds

1 garlic clove, minced

6 tablespoons plain Greek-style yogurt

Juice of ½ lime

Fine sea salt and freshly ground pepper

Preheat the oven to 400°F (200°C).

Toss the vegetables in a large mixing bowl with 2 tablespoons of the olive oil.

Set a small, dry skillet over medium-high heat, and fry the coriander and cumin seeds for a couple of minutes, until they begin to pop in the pan, and smell aromatic. Grind the seeds in a mortar using a pestle; add the spices to the vegetables and toss to combine. Add the garlic, yogurt, lime juice, and salt and pepper to taste and stir again. Spread vegetables in a roasting pan and drizzle with the remaining tablespoon of olive oil. Cover the pan with foil, and bake for about 50 minutes, or until the vegetables are beautifully soft and the yogurt has reduced to a crumbly, spicy coating.

Root Vegetable Bake

This is a dish you really cannot overcook: the thinly sliced root vegetables simmer away until they're tender and have absorbed the orange-scented stock. It's great for quickly assembling at lunchtime and popping in the oven a couple of hours before dinner.

Serves 4 to 6

1 pound (400 grams) waxy potatoes, such as round white or red potatoes

12 ounces (300 grams) carrots

12 ounces (300 grams) celery root

5 tablespoons (75 milliliters) olive oil

Juice of 1 orange (about ½ cup or 120 milliliters)

¾ cup (200 milliliters) vegetable stock

1 tablespoon chopped fresh cilantro (coriander)

Fine sea salt and freshly ground pepper

Preheat the oven to 375°F (190°C).

Peel all the vegetables and cut into very thin slices, about ⅛-inch thick.

Bring a small pot with an inch of water to boil. Add the carrot slices and cook for 2 minutes, just to heat through. Drain and reserve.

Drizzle a little of the oil over the base of a large, ovenproof casserole about 9 inches in diameter. Put a layer of potato slices in the bottom of the casserole, followed by a layer of carrots, and a layer of celery root, adding a splash of oil to each layer. Repeat the process, finishing with a final layer of potato.

Mix the orange juice with the stock and cilantro; season with salt and pepper, then pour over the vegetables.

Cover the casserole and bake for 1 ½ hours, until the vegetables feel beautifully soft when pierced with a knife. Remove the lid for the final 30 minutes cooking time.

Parsnip and Apple Fritters

As an alternative to roasted parsnips, you could serve these fritters with a joint of meat, or enjoy them as a snack with Hazelnut Cream Cheese (page 162).

Serves 4

1 ½ pounds (700 grams) whole parsnips

2 dessert apples (such as Jonagold or Golden Delicious),
    peeled, cored, and grated,

1-inch piece fresh ginger, peeled and minced

¼ cup (30 grams) all-purpose flour, plus more as needed

1 large egg, beaten

2 tablespoons butter, at room temperature

3 tablespoons chopped fresh parsley

Fine sea salt and freshly ground pepper

2 tablespoons olive oil

Preheat the oven to 400°F (200°C). Grease a large baking sheet.

Peel and quarter the parsnips, and remove the woody core. Fill a pot with an inch of water, and set over medium heat to boil. Add the parsnips and cook for 2 to 3 minutes, until just barely tender but firm enough to grate. Drain well and cool briefly, then coarsely grate the parsnips into a large bowl. Alternatively, use the grating attachment on a food processor.

Add all the remaining ingredients except the olive oil. Stir well to combine, and season with salt and pepper.

With floured hands, take a spoonful of the mixture and press it into a little cake in your hands, about 3 inches across and 1-inch thick. Don't try to be too neat: think rustic. Place the cake on the prepared baking sheet and repeat until you have used all the mixture, giving you about 8 cakes.

Drizzle the cakes with the olive oil and bake for 30 minutes, turning the cakes over after 15 minutes, until the tops are golden and crispy.

Parsnips

By late winter, the good old reliable parsnip comes into its own, and although I hate washing the icy, muddy brutes I am so glad to have them. Sweetened by a good hard frost, they are a truly versatile winter staple, a great ingredient in soups, and a cornerstone of Christmas dinner. Older parsnips may have a woody core which should be cut out before cooking.

Shredded Brussels Sprouts with Chorizo

I'm a bit of a purist where Brussels sprouts are concerned. As long as they are really fresh, I adore them simply steamed, and so do two of my three children. Usually, it is definitely not worth meddling with such a healthy state of affairs. I do break the rule for this recipe though, which is a nice combination of smoky, spiced sausage and sweet, nutty sprouts. It's also a great way to use up sprouts that have opened more fully and are leafier around the outside. This is delicious alongside rice dishes.

Serves 4

12 ounces (300 grams) Brussels sprouts, preferably
   leafy and not so tightly closed

4 ounces (100 grams) Spanish semi-cured chorizo,
   casings removed

Sea salt and freshly ground pepper

Thinly slice the Brussels sprouts, or use a slicing attachment in a food processor. Cut the chorizo into ½-inch chunks.

Set a large skillet over high heat. Add the chorizo

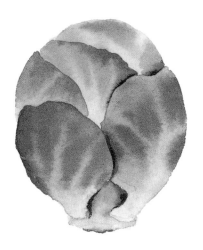

and sauté until the fat starts to render. Add the sliced sprouts and stir well to combine. Cover and reduce the heat to a moderate level, and cook for about 5 minutes. Give the pan a shake now and then to ensure even cooking, and lift the lid to make sure the sprouts are not overcooked. If they are beginning to stick to the pan, add a couple of tablespoons of water. They should be cooked through but not soggy.

The sprouts may not need any further seasoning if the chorizo was good and spicy, but taste, and add salt and pepper, if necessary.

Red Cabbage with Marmalade

Traditionally, red cabbage is given a steamy, spicy, sweet-and-sour twist. I rather like this lazy alternative which steeps the cabbage in citrus, giving it a more subtle flavor that goes well with roast meats.

Serves 6

2 tablespoons olive oil

4 large shallots, thinly sliced

½ red cabbage, sliced into long, thin strips

2 tablespoons good-quality orange marmalade

Fine sea salt and freshly ground pepper

Preheat oven to 300°F (150°C).

Heat the olive oil in a Dutch oven (or heavy, oven-safe pan with a tightly fitting lid) set over medium-low heat. Add the shallots and sauté gently until they are translucent. Add the sliced cabbage and marmalade and season with salt and pepper. Give the cabbage a good stir to combine, then cover and bake for about 1½ hours, until the cabbage is thoroughly cooked but still has a bit of a "bite" to it. The cabbage should cook in its own juices, but check every half hour and if it looks a bit dry add a couple tablespoons of water.

Winter Coleslaw with Fennel and Pear

Sliced very thinly, red cabbage makes a crunchy and colorful salad. Fennel and pear provide the contrast of spicy licorice and ripe fruit. This salad is best tossed together just before serving to keep the cabbage from bleeding purple onto the fennel and pear.

Serves 4 to 6

½ head red cabbage, cored

1 fennel bulb, fronds removed

1 tablespoon freshly squeezed lemon juice

2 ripe Comice or Williams (Bartlett) pears

4 tablespoons mayonnaise

4 tablespoons low fat crème fraîche or plain Greek-style yogurt

1 tablespoon chopped fresh cilantro (coriander)

Fine sea salt and freshly ground pepper

Slice the cabbage as thinly as possible, or use a food processor with a shredding attachment to yield thin strips. Transfer to a large mixing bowl.

Cut the fennel bulb in half lengthwise, then set the flat side down on the chopping board. Slice thinly into long shreds. Toss in a separate bowl with the lemon juice.

Peel, core, and quarter the pears. Cut each piece lengthwise into thin slices, and add to the fennel.

Mix the mayonnaise and crème frâiche together, pour over the cabbage, and mix thoroughly. Add the fennel-pear mixture and the cilantro, season to taste with salt and pepper, and stir lightly to combine.

Onion and Celery Soup

This is a chunky soup, which combines the sweetness of slow-cooked onions with the bitterness of celery. It's not a quick one, but once the vegetables are chopped you can forget about it; the flavors slowly intensify during a long simmer. I've added a swirl of cream at the end, but it can easily be omitted. This is delicious with a thick slice of toast spread with Hazelnut Cream Cheese (page 162).

Serves 4

2 large onions

6 ribs celery

½ cup (115 grams) unsalted butter

4 garlic cloves, thinly sliced

Fine sea salt and freshly ground pepper

2 medium waxy potatoes, such as round white or red (about 12 ounces or 300 grams)

2 cups (475 milliliters) hot vegetable stock

Freshly grated nutmeg, for serving

4 tablespoons heavy whipping cream, for serving (optional)

Quarter the onions and slice very thinly. Slice the celery in half the length of the stalk, then chop into thin slices across the grain.

Melt the butter in a large skillet over medium heat. Add the onions, celery, and garlic, and stir well to coat everything evenly with the butter. Season with salt and pepper. Reduce the heat to its lowest setting. Tuck a sheet of aluminum foil directly over the vegetables and let them sweat slowly for 45 minutes.

Peel and dice the potato into small cubes. Add the diced potatoes to the skillet, stir to combine, and press the foil down on the vegetables, keeping the heat low. Simmer for another 40 minutes, or until the potato is tender. Add a couple of tablespoons of stock if the vegetables are beginning to stick to the skillet.

Transfer the vegetables to a large pot, add the stock, and heat through over medium heat; check the seasoning and add salt and pepper to taste.

To serve, divide the soup among 4 warmed bowls, and finish with a swirl of cream and a grating of nutmeg.

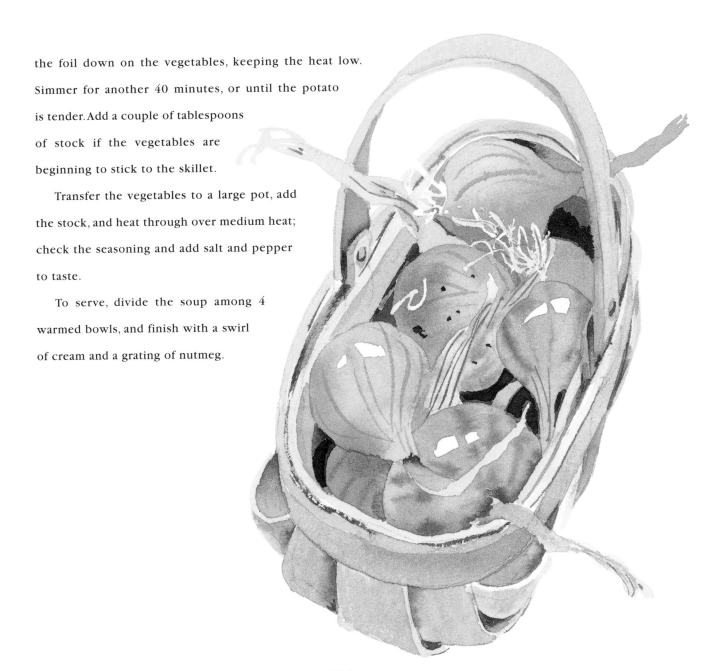

Red Onion Yorkshire Puddings

Yorkshire puddings are a must with roast beef; it's lovely to find a puddle of syrupy red onions lurking in the base of each golden puff. Or they can become a meal in themselves with the addition of a couple of cubes of goat cheese along with the onions in the batter. Both the onions and the batter can be made ahead of time, even the day before. Just leave the batter in a covered bowl in the fridge overnight.

Makes 6 to 8

CARAMELIZED ONIONS

1 tablespoon unsalted butter

3 medium red onions, finely diced

A sprinkling of chopped fresh thyme

1 teaspoon maple syrup or honey

Fine sea salt and freshly ground pepper

BATTER

¾ cup (100 grams) all-purpose flour

Pinch salt

3 large eggs

1 cup (300 milliliters) milk

3 teaspoons beef drippings or butter

Preheat the oven to 400°F (200°C).

For the onions: Melt the butter in an ovenproof baking dish, then add all the remaining ingredients and stir well to combine. Cover and roast in the oven for 30 to 40 minutes, until the onions are tender and glossy. Check and stir occasionally, as cooking times may vary. Remove from the oven and set aside; maintain oven temperature.

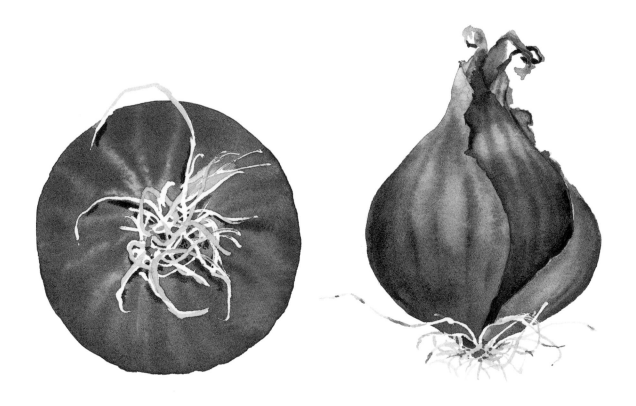

For the batter: Combine the flour and salt in a mixing bowl. Make a well in the center and break the eggs into it. Using a whisk or an electric mixer on medium speed, gradually beat the eggs into the flour, adding the milk little by little as the batter gets thick and sticky. Continue to beat until the batter is smooth.

Put ½ teaspoon drippings in each compartment of a 6-count deep pudding or muffin tray. If you're making 8 puddings, use two 4-ounce ramekins additionally. Set the tray and ramekins, if using, in the oven for a couple of minutes to heat the drippings until they just begin to smoke. Remove the tray from the oven and quickly divide the batter among the compartments; it should sizzle as it hits the fat. Add a spoonful of onions to each one and put the tray straight back in the oven. Bake for 30 minutes, until they are beautifully risen and golden. Resist opening the oven door while they are cooking or they will collapse. Serve hot.

Caramelized Onion Dumplings

Baked in individual dariole or baba molds (or you could use ramekins or custard cups), these dumplings are a savory take on treacle pudding: little mounds of sage and walnut sponge topped with succulent caramelized onions. They make a light vegetarian lunch served with a goat cheese salad, or happily accompany a hearty winter casserole. The onions take a while to cook, but can be prepared in advance and kept in the refrigerator for a few days.

Serves 4

CARAMELIZED ONIONS

2 tablespoons butter

2 large onions, thinly sliced

½ teaspoon salt

1 tablespoon granulated sugar

DUMPLINGS

½ cup (50 grams) chopped walnuts

1 cup (130 grams) self-rising flour

2 teaspoons baking powder

½ cup (115 grams) unsalted butter, at room temperature

2 large eggs, lightly beaten

2 tablespoons milk

6 fresh sage leaves, finely chopped, or 1 teaspoon dried sage

For the onions: Melt the butter in a large, heavy skillet over medium heat. Add the onions, salt, and sugar. Stir well to incorporate, then press a sheet of foil directly onto the onions. Reduce the heat to the lowest setting and let the onions cook very gently for about 40 to 50 minutes, stirring occasionally. The onions should be beautifully soft and glossy. Remove the foil and continue to cook for a couple of minutes to reduce any excess liquid. Remove from the heat but leave in the pan while you prepare the dumplings.

For the dumplings: Preheat the oven to 350°F (180°C). Grease 8 individual dariole molds or ramekins.

Using a mortar and pestle, crush the walnuts until they are grainy or put the nuts in a resealable plastic bag and crush with a rolling pin.

Combine the flour, baking powder, butter, eggs, milk, and sage in a mixing bowl and beat with an electric mixer until smooth. Fold in the walnuts.

Divide the onions among the molds or ramekins, then top with the dumpling mixture. Bake for 20 minutes, until well-risen and springy to the touch, or until a tester comes out with only a few crumbs clinging to it. They may sink slightly when you take them out of the oven. Invert the dumplings onto plates to serve.

Braised Beef with Chorizo and Celery

After making my Christmas puddings I usually have a few spare cans of stout in the pantry. Added to this stew, they bring out the depth of flavor in the beef, which should be very tender after a long, slow cooking. As with all slowly braised meat dishes, this one is well-suited to making in advance and reheating. I like to serve it with a seasonal potato-and-parsnip mash.

Serves 4 to 6

2 tablespoons unsalted butter

1 cup (150 grams) chopped celery (about 4 medium ribs)

1 cup (150 grams) chopped onion (1 medium)

¾ cup (125 grams) good-quality Spanish dry-cured chorizo,
    cut into ¼-inch slices

2 tablespoons all-purpose flour

2¼ pounds (1 kilogram) cubed stewing beef

1 tablespoon olive oil

4 bay leaves

1 tablespoon dried thyme (or ½ tablespoon chopped fresh)

12 ounces (330 milliliters) stout or other dark beer

1¼ cups (300 milliliters) beef stock, plus more as needed

Fine sea salt and freshly ground pepper

Preheat oven to 325°F (170°C).

Melt the butter in a medium skillet over medium heat and gently sauté the celery, onions, and chorizo until the vegetables are softened, about 5 minutes. Transfer vegetable mixture to a large, lidded casserole and reserve skillet.

Place the flour in a large paper or plastic bag, then add the beef. Holding it tightly closed, give the bag a good shake to coat the beef with the flour.

Add the olive oil to the reserved skillet set over medium heat. Brown the meat, in batches if necessary, on all sides, and transfer to the casserole. Add all remaining ingredients to the casserole with the beef and vegetables; stir to combine, cover, and put into the oven. You can almost forget about the casserole for at least 2½ to 3 hours, or until the beef is tender and falling apart. Check the liquid levels towards the end of the cooking time, and add more stock or water if the dish looks too dry.

Root Vegetable Tarte Tatin

This is a great vegetarian dish making the most of melt-in-the mouth root vegetables. I like to serve it with a contrasting crunchy Winter Coleslaw (page 233). You can substitute about 12 ounces or 300 grams of store-bought puff pastry for the Rich Shortbread Pastry.

Serves 4

RICH SHORTBREAD PASTRY

1 ½ cups (180 grams) all-purpose flour

Pinch fine sea salt

¼ cup (60 grams) very cold unsalted butter

¼ cup (60 grams) very cold vegetable shortening

1 tablespoon chopped fresh marjoram

1 large egg yolk

3 tablespoons very cold water

FILLING

6 to 8 shallots

1 ½ pounds (750 grams) root vegetables (carrots, parsnips, celery root, small potatoes, or sweet potatoes)

2 tablespoons olive oil

1-inch piece fresh ginger, peeled and very finely sliced

1 ¼ cups (300 milliliters) vegetable stock

1 tablespoon chopped fresh marjoram leaves

3 tablespoons melted unsalted butter

1 tablespoon castor (superfine) sugar

Fine sea salt and freshly ground pepper

Preheat the oven to 400°F (200°C).

For the shortbread pastry: Sift the flour and salt into a bowl. Chop the butter and shortening into small pieces, then rub into the flour with your fingers until it resembles coarse breadcrumbs. Add the marjoram.

In a small bowl, beat the egg yolk with the water, then gradually add it to the flour, mixing with a fork to combine. You may not need to add all the liquid; use just enough to bind the flour until it forms a stiff dough.

Transfer the dough to a floured board and roll out a circle of pastry slightly bigger in diameter than a large, ovenproof skillet approximately 10 inches in diameter. Transfer the dough to a floured baking sheet cover with plastic wrap and refrigerate while you prepare the vegetables.

For the filling: Halve the shallots lengthwise and peel off the outer layers of skin. Peel the root vegetables and cut into chunks roughly the same size as the shallot halves (cuts on the diagonal look nice).

Heat the olive oil in a heavy, ovenproof skillet over medium heat, then add the ginger and the vegetables and sauté for 2 to 3 minutes, stirring occasionally to brown all sides. Add the stock and the chopped marjoram and simmer for 10 to 15 minutes, or until the stock has evaporated and the vegetables are beginning to soften. Add the melted butter and sugar and stir gently.

Lay the cold pastry over the vegetables in the skillet like a lid, tucking the edges down over the vegetables on the inside rim.

Bake for about 25 minutes, by which time the top should be beautifully golden. Invert onto a plate to serve.

Mussels with Shallots and Parsley

After several failed attempts, I now have a couple of thriving clumps of curly parsley established in the garden. If I keep it covered with a cloche as the weather cools, I can just about pick right through the depths of winter. With parsley at the ready and a good crop of shallots in store, I eagerly await the arrival of the mussel season. Around November, the Friday fish van brings in the first incredibly sweet and tender mussels, harvested from local waters. Friday night becomes Mussels Night and invariably eclipses the chill of winter with memories of moules frites eaten in sunny Mediterranean harbor-side restaurants. An incredibly quick and easy supper, this is best served with chunky homemade brown bread to mop up the juices or Lemon-Garlic Oven Fries (page 224) with Mayonnaise (page 56).

Serves 4

4 pounds (2 kilograms) mussels

3 tablespoons butter

4 ounces (80 grams) shallots, finely chopped (about ½ cup)

1 garlic clove, finely chopped

3 tablespoons chopped fresh parsley, divided

1 cup (250 milliliters) dry white wine

½ cup (120 milliliters) heavy whipping cream (substitiute double cream)

Clean the mussels thoroughly by scrubbing each one with a brush under running water. Pull off the beards with a good tug, and discard any shells that are not tightly shut.

Melt the butter in a very large stockpot over medium heat; later you will

244

need room for all the mussels plus enough space to give them a good shake. When the butter is foaming, add the shallots and garlic and cook for 5 minutes, until both are softened. Add 2 tablespoons parsley, the wine, and the mussels. Cover and increase the heat to medium-high. Cook for about 4 to 5 minutes, giving the pan a good shake every now and again. The mussels will steam open; any that remain closed should be discarded. Stir in the cream and keep on the heat for about 30 seconds, just long enough to heat it through.

Spoon out the mussels into 4 large warmed bowls, then strain the liquid through a fine sieve before distributing it among each bowl. Sprinkle with the remaining tablespoon of parsley and serve immediately.

Don't forget to put an extra empty bowl on the table for the shells.

Slow-Cooked Rabbit with Mustard and Thyme

Inspired by a wonderful rabbit casserole eaten in Provence almost twenty years ago, this recipe combines Dijon mustard with the sweet flesh of celeriac, or celery root, and parsnip, both of which are at their best in early winter. This recipe serves two generously, but even better, save some of the meat and any leftover sauce for Rabbit Risotto (page 248) the following day. I like to serve this with creamy mashed potatoes.

Serves 2 with ample leftovers

5 tablespoons sunflower oil, divided

1 large onion, cut into thick slices

6 tablespoons (40 grams) all-purpose flour

Sea salt and freshly ground pepper

½ celery root (about 13 ounces or 375 grams), cut into 2-inch chunks

1 medium parsnip (about 6 ounces or 150 grams), cut into 2-inch chunks

1 (2½-pound) rabbit (ask your butcher to joint it for you, and include the liver)

1½ cups (350 milliliters) dry white wine

1½ cups (350 milliliters) vegetable stock, heated and kept warm

1 tablespoon Dijon mustard

1 tablespoon fresh thyme leaves or ½ tablespoon dried

Preheat oven to 325°F (170°C).

Melt 3 tablespoons of the oil in a large skillet over medium heat. Add the onion, and cook for 5 minutes, until softened, stirring occasionally.

Put the flour in a mixing bowl and season with salt and pepper. Add the celery root and parsnip, and toss until all the pieces are coated with the flour. Transfer the vegetables (reserving the excess flour) to the skillet with the onion and cook for about 5 minutes, turning regularly with a spatula until the flour smells toasty and the vegetables begin to brown on the edges. Scrape all the vegetables into a large casserole dish.

Toss the rabbit pieces, including the liver, in the remaining flour. Heat the remaining 2 tablespoons of oil in the skillet over high heat, add the rabbit pieces, in batches if necessary, and briefly brown on all sides. Transfer the rabbit meat to a cutting board or plate. Chop the liver finely and transfer to the casserole along with the rest of the rabbit.

Pour the wine and vegetable stock into the casserole. Add the mustard and the thyme and stir to incorporate. Cover and bake for 2½ hours, stirring halfway through cooking, until the meat is tender and the sauce is thick and peppery. Adjust seasoning to taste and serve.

Rabbit Risotto

I am a firm believer in leftovers. My first rabbit risotto came about like a phoenix from the ashes of a rabbit casserole: not much rabbit, but heaps of delicious mustardy stock. The rice absorbed the stock and made a richly flavored and creamy risotto. This adaptation of that happy accident combines the fresh flavor of celery with gamey rabbit meat.

Serves 4

3 tablespoons unsalted butter

3 or 4 shallots, finely chopped

2 to 3 ribs celery, finely chopped

1½ cups (350 grams) Arborio rice

1 cup plus 1 tablespoon (200 milliliters) dry white wine

8 ounces (200 grams) cooked rabbit meat,
 coarsely chopped (leftovers are perfect)

2 tablespoons chopped fresh flat-leaf parsley

4½ cups (1 liter) vegetable stock, heated and kept warm

¼ cup (30 grams) freshly grated Parmesan cheese, divided

2 tablespoons heavy whipping cream

Fine sea salt and freshly ground pepper

Extra-virgin olive oil for drizzling

Melt the butter in a large, deep skillet over medium-low heat. Add the shallots and the celery and sauté for 5 minutes, or until soft. Add the rice and stir with a wooden spoon to coat the grains with butter. Toast the grains for 2 minutes.

Stir in the wine and leave to bubble gently until nearly all the wine has evaporated. Add the rabbit meat and the parsley, then begin adding the stock a cup at a time, stirring regularly. Only add more stock once the previous cup has been absorbed by the rice. After 15 to 20 minutes the grains should be slightly al dente,

but very creamy. You may have some stock left over.

Stir in 2 tablespoons of the Parmesan and the cream. Season with salt and pepper to taste, and let the cream heat through for a few seconds. Serve immediately on deep, warmed plates. Drizzle a little olive oil over each and finish with a sprinkling of the remaining Parmesan.

Rabbit

Rabbit is a frequent topic of conversation among country gardeners, though less in terms of recipe swapping and more in terms of how to keep the blighters from feasting on your seedlings. We have largely solved the problem by having three wily cats that patrol by night and enjoy the best possible free-range, organic diet that exists. During the game season our excellent butcher sells local wild rabbit, so the least I can do is cook a few and save a row or two of broad beans in the process. Rabbit is very lean with a fine texture, similar to chicken but with a stronger gamey taste, and is suited to long, slow cooking until it falls off the bone.

Apple-Ginger Meringue Cake

A cake base studded with pieces of candied ginger is topped with tender apples slices and a crown of soft-centered meringue.

Serves 6 to 8

½ cup (115 grams) butter, at room temperature

1 cup (200 grams) castor (superfine) sugar, divided,

     plus 2 tablespoons (25 grams) for sprinkling

1 ¾ cups (200 grams) self-rising flour

2 large eggs, separated

5 tablespoons (75 grams) candied ginger, finely chopped

12 ounces (350 grams) baking apples (about 2 medium apples)

Preheat the oven to 325°F (170°C). Grease and line an 8-inch cake pan (preferably springform) with a removable bottom with a circle of parchment paper.

Combine the butter, ½ cup (100 grams) sugar, flour, and egg yolks in a mixing bowl. Using an electric mixer, beat on low speed to combine all the ingredients. Stir in the candied ginger. Spread the mixture over the bottom of the cake pan.

Peel, core, and slice the apples about ⅛-inch thick, and pile on top of the cake batter in the pan. Sprinkle with the 2 tablespoons of sugar.

Place the egg whites in very clean, dry mixing bowl, and beat with an electric mixer on high speed until they form stiff peaks, about 2 minutes. Beat in half of the remaining sugar until the peaks are stiff and glossy, about 1 minute, then fold in the remainder with a spatula.

Carefully spread the meringue evenly over the apples, making sure it touches the side of the pan all the way around.

Bake for 40 to 45 minutes, by which time the meringue should be golden and crusty on top and the apples tender inside.

Leave in the pan to cool for at least 5 minutes before attempting to slide the base out of the pan.

251

Black Currant Crumble Tarts

These are nice made as individual tarts if you have a tray that makes four 4-inch tarts; otherwise, use a single 8-inch round pan with a removable bottom. Make sure you have some cream on hand to pour over the warm tarts.

Serves 4

PASTRY

¾ cup (100 grams) all-purpose flour

Pinch salt

2 tablespoons unsalted butter, chilled

2 tablespoons vegetable shortening, chilled

1 large egg yolk

3 tablespoons ice water

FILLING

2 tablespoons unsalted butter

8 ounces (200 grams) black currants (fresh or frozen)

¾ cup (150 grams) castor (superfine) sugar

CRUMBLE TOPPING

3 tablespoons unsalted butter, chilled

⅓ cup, plus 1 tablespoon (60 grams) all-purpose flour

½ cup (50 grams) rolled oats

¼ cup (50 grams) castor (superfine) sugar

Preheat the oven to 350°F (180°C). Grease a suitable 4-tart tray or 8-inch round tart pan.

For the pastry: Sift together the flour and salt into a bowl. Chop the butter and shortening into small cubes and rub them into the flour with the tips of your fingers, until the mixture resembles breadcrumbs. Beat the egg yolk with the ice water then begin slowly adding it to the flour, mixing with a fork to combine. You may not need to add all the liquid; rather, just enough to bind the flour into a dough.

On a floured board, roll the pastry out to between ¼- and ⅛-inch thick. Cut out pastry circle(s) to cover the bottom and sides of the pan(s) you are using, and into the bottom. Transfer to the refrigerator to chill while you make the rest of the components.

For the filling: Melt the butter in a small saucepan over medium heat and add the black currants and sugar, stirring until the sugar has dissolved. Simmer for about 8 to 10 minutes, or until you have a thick, glossy sauce. Set aside.

For the topping: Measure all the ingredients into a mixing bowl. Using your hands or an electric mixer on a low speed, rub the butter into the flour, oats, and sugar until the mixture resembles coarse breadcrumbs.

Divide the black currant filling among the tarts or pour it into the large tart pan, then top with the crumble mixture.

Bake for 25 minutes, or until the crumble topping is golden-brown. Leave to cool in the pan for 5 minutes before attempting to cut. Serve while still warm.

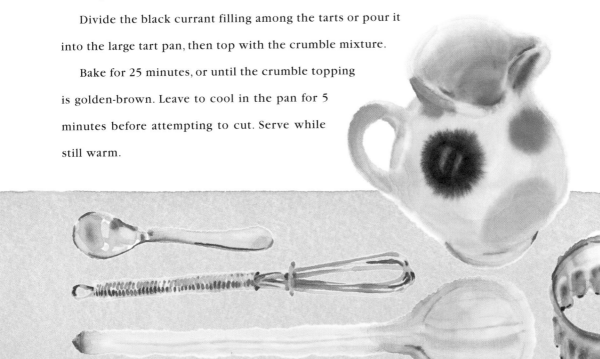

Black Currant and Almond-Baked Apple

This is a perfect winter dish of steaming, soft apple, with a deliciously sticky core of ground almonds and black currants. Use a good baking apple that holds its shape, such as Jonagold. The quantities here are for one apple, so you can adapt it easily for however many people you are feeding. I use frozen black currants in the winter, but you could also substitute blueberries.

Serves 1

1 tablespoon butter

1 tablespoon Demerara-style raw sugar

¼ cup (25 grams) ground almonds (almond meal)

1 ounce (25 grams) black currants

1 teaspoon honey

1 baking apple

. . . .

Preheat the oven to 350°C (180°F).

Put the butter in a small, ovenproof mixing bowl and pop it into the hot oven for a couple of minutes to melt. Add the sugar, ground almonds, black currants, and honey to the melted butter and mix well with a fork, squashing the currants as you do so.

Score the skin right around the middle of the apple, to prevent it from bursting. Remove the core, leaving a 1½-inch opening. (My corer makes a very small channel, so I carve away with a knife to make it bigger.)

Place the apple in a greased baking dish, stuff the core with the currant mixture, and place it in the oven. Bake for 30 to 40 minutes, or until the flesh is tender when pierced with a knife. Keep an eye on it towards the end of the cooking time; the apple will begin to disintegrate if overcooked.

Cool for 5 minutes before serving, otherwise you are guaranteed to burn your tongue. (That's just enough time to whip up some custard.)

Black Currants

Black currants have an intense, sharp flavor, and when cooked turn deliciously syrupy. Their relatively tough skins make them perfect for freezing. Don't even bother to stem them; it's much easier to shake off the stems once the berries are frozen. I've included black currants in the winter section, as a reminder to trawl through the freezer to find the remnants of summer sunshine.

Black Currant Mousse

This is simply smooth, fruity, creamy, deep-pink gorgeousness. If you want a bit of crunch to go with it, try Crisp Butter Biscuits (page 49). This recipe works equally well with fresh or frozen fruit.

Serves 4

4 ounces (100 grams) black currants

½ cup (100 grams) castor (superfine) sugar

2 sheets gelatin

1 cup (200 milliliters) heavy whipping cream

. . . .

Put the black currants in a saucepan with 1 cup (200 milliliters) water. Add the sugar and set the pan over medium-low heat. Cook the black currants, stirring occasionally, for 5 minutes, or until tender. Remove from the heat and leave in the pan.

Soak the gelatin sheets in cold water for 5 minutes, or until soft. Squeeze out the excess water, then gradually add them to the hot black currants, stirring to dissolve. Set aside to cool to room temperature.

Using an electric mixer, whip the cream in a large mixing bowl on medium speed until it forms soft peaks. Gradually fold in the black currant mixture with a spatula until fully combined. Pour the mousse into individual dessert bowls or a pretty serving bowl.

Orchard Chutney

The recipe for any chutney is roughly the same: a mixture of fruits, vegetables, vinegar, sugar, and spices, slowly simmered until gloriously thick and tangy. Using the same proportions, you can adapt it to deal with whatever is ripe in the garden, and begging for attention. For a chunky chutney I use Howgate Wonder, (or Idared). For a sloppier texture I would use McIntosh or Bramleys, as they won't disintegrate when cooked.

Makes five 12-ounce (340 gram) jars

1 pound (450 grams) cooking apples, peeled, cored, and chopped

1 pound (450 grams) butternut squash (or similar squash), peeled and chopped

1 pound (450 grams) onions (about 2 large), finely chopped

1 pound (450 grams) golden raisins

1 ½ cups (300 grams) dark brown muscovado sugar or packed dark brown sugar

1 ¼ cups (300 milliliters) white wine vinegar

6 cloves

1 teaspoon black peppercorns

1-inch piece fresh unpeeled bruised ginger, (just give it a bash with a rolling pin)

Fine sea salt and freshly ground pepper

Prepare five 12-ounce glass canning jars by washing and sterilizing them. (See page 61 for instructions.)

Combine the apples, squash, and onions in a large stockpot along with the raisins, sugar, and vinegar.

Tie the cloves, peppercorns, and ginger in a little muslin bag. Where's the muslin bag when you need it? You can also improvise with a corner of cheesecloth or clean kitchen towel. Add the spice bag to the pot.

Set the pot over medium heat and stir the chutney until the sugar has dissolved and the mixture is bubbling. Reduce the heat to low and simmer for about an hour, stirring occasionally, until the mixture looks like. . . chutney! The longer you cook it, the thicker it will become, so be careful not to let it burn on the bottom of the pan towards the end of cooking. Reduce the heat if necessary. Taste and season with salt and pepper.

Spoon into the sterilized glass jars. Screw on the metal lids while still hot, and allow to cool on the counter. The chutney will keep, unopened, in a cool, dry place for 1 year or opened, in the refrigerator, for 4 months.

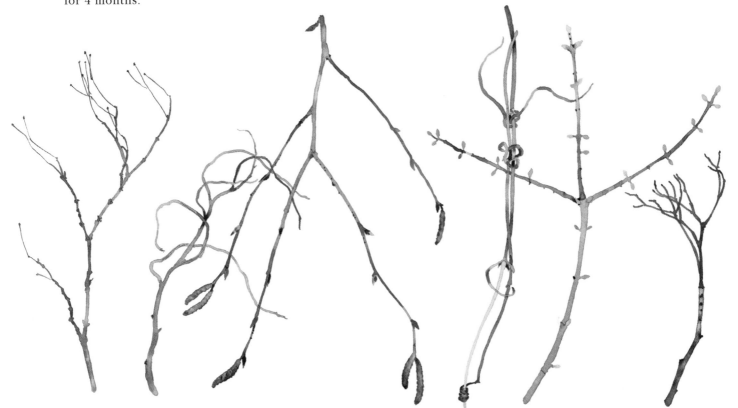

Balsamic Pear and Beet Relish

According to Ralph Waldo Emerson, "There are only ten minutes in the life of a pear when it is perfect to eat." Even if you're lucky enough to get your pears from a local farm stand, the entire pear crop is likely to be ripe in the same ten minutes, and there are only so many pears one can eat! This richly colored compote will use up a few, and it's great served warm with a juicy pork chop or cold with crumbly cheeses. Stored in the fridge, it will keep for about a week.

Makes four 10-ounce (300 milliliter) jars

3 beets (about 500 grams)

2 tablespoons olive oil

4 pears, not over-ripe, peeled, cored, and cut into small chunks

2 tablespoons unsalted butter, melted

2 tablespoons dark brown muscovado sugar

1 tablespoon balsamic vinegar

Fine sea salt and freshly ground pepper

Preheat the oven to 350°F (180°C).

Wash the beets well, leaving the root intact, and twist off the tops without damaging the skin. Wrap each beet in a large square of aluminum foil and bake for about an hour until easily pierced with a knife. Raise the oven temperature to 375°F (190°C).

When cool enough to handle, dice the beets. (You should have 3 cups.) Place the beets in a roasting pan large enough for the chunks to lie in a single layer and drizzle them with the olive oil. Bake for about

15 minutes, by which time they should be sizzling. Add the pears, melted butter, sugar, and balsamic vinegar to the roasting pan. Season to taste with salt and pepper and stir gently to combine. Continue to bake for 15 minutes more, by which time the beet and pear should begin to caramelize around the edges.

Serve warm from the oven or store in the refrigerator in glass canning jars (see page 61 for preparing the jars).

Conversion Tables

FORMULAS FOR
METRIC CONVERSION

Ounces to grams	multiply ounces by 28.35
Pounds to grams	multiply pounds by 453.5
Cups to liters	multiply cups by .24
Fahrenheit to Centigrade	subtract 32 from Fahrenheit, multiply by 5 and divide by 9

METRIC EQUIVALENTS FOR VOLUME

U.S.	Metric		U.S.	Metric	
$1/8$ tsp.	0.6 ml		$1/3$ cup	79 ml	
$1/4$ tsp.	1.2 ml		$1/2$ cup	118 ml	4 fl. oz
$1/2$ tsp.	2.5 ml		$2/3$ cup	158 ml	
$3/4$ tsp.	3.7 ml		$3/4$ cup	178 ml	6 fl. oz
1 tsp.	5 ml		1 cup	237 ml	8 fl. oz
$1 1/2$ tsp.	7.4 ml		$1 1/4$ cups	300 ml	
2 tsp.	10 ml		$1 1/2$ cups	355 ml	
1 Tbsp.	15 ml		$1 3/4$ cups	425 ml	
$1 1/2$ Tbsp.	22 ml		2 cups (1 pint)	500 ml	16 fl. oz
2 Tbsp. ($1/8$ cup)	30 ml	1 fl. oz	3 cups	725 ml	
3 Tbsp.	45 ml		1 quart	.95 liters	32 fl. oz
$1/4$ cup	59 ml	2 fl. oz	1 gallon	3.8 liters	128 fl. oz

METRIC EQUIVALENTS FOR BUTTER

U.S.	Metric
2 tsp.	10 g
1 Tbsp.	15 g
1½ Tbsp.	22.5 g
2 Tbsp.	27 g
3 Tbsp.	42 g
4 Tbsp.	56 g
4 oz. (1 stick)	110 g
8 oz. (2 sticks)	220 g

METRIC EQUIVALENTS FOR LENGTH

U.S.	Metric
¼ inch	.65 cm
½ inch	1.25 cm
1 inch	2.50 cm
2 inches	5.00 cm
3 inches	6.00 cm
4 inches	8.00 cm
5 inches	11.00 cm
6 inches	15.00 cm
7 inches	18.00 cm
8 inches	20.00 cm
9 inches	23.00 cm
12 inches	30.50 cm
15 inches	38.00 cm

OVEN TEMPERATURES

Degrees Fahrenheit	Degrees Centigrade	British Gas Marks
200°	93°	—
250°	120°	½
275°	140°	1
300°	150°	2
325°	165°	3
350°	175°	4
375°	190°	5
400°	200°	6
450°	230°	8

METRIC EQUIVALENTS FOR WEIGHT

U.S.	Metric
1 oz	28 g
2 oz	57 g
3 oz	85 g
4 oz (¼ lb.)	113 g
5 oz	142 g
6 oz	170 g
7 oz	198 g
8 oz (½ lb.)	227 g
1 lb.	454 g

Source: Herbst, Sharon Tyler. *The Food Lover's Companion.* 3rd ed. Hauppauge: Barron's, 2001.

Index

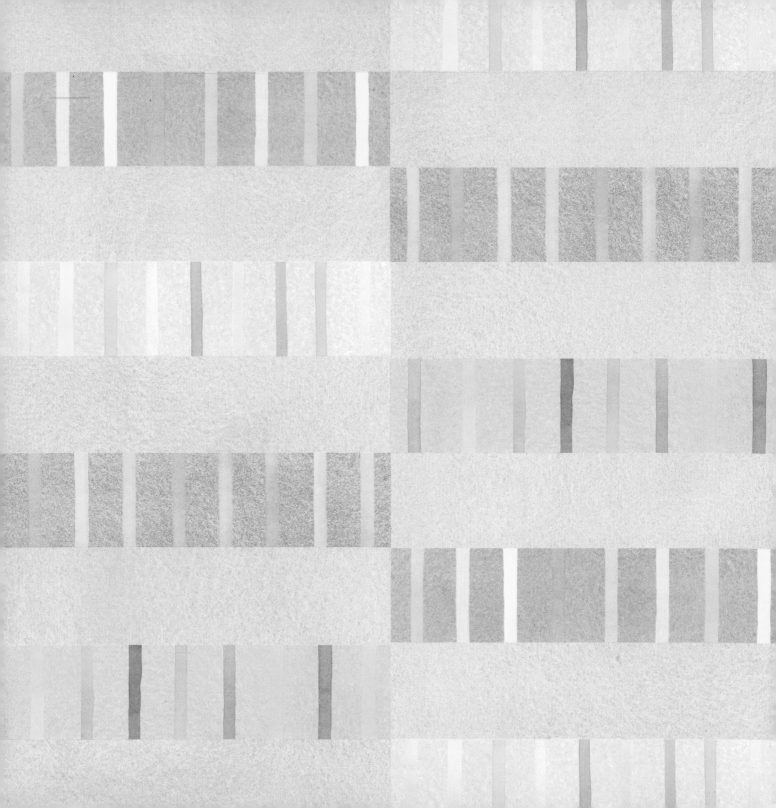